For Ken -
In appreciation for your
wise counsel + support.
Best regards,
Art

FOUR-FINGER SINGER AND HIS LATE WIFE, KATE

A Nov
of
Life, Death & Baseball

ARTHUR D. HITTNER

Apple Ridge Press
Oro Valley, AZ

ISBN 978-0-9989810-4-8

Cover Design by Pure Fusion Media
Formatting by Polgarus Studio

ALSO BY
ARTHUR D. HITTNER

FICTION

Artist, Soldier, Lover, Muse

NON-FICTION

Honus Wagner:
The Life of Baseball's 'Flying Dutchman'

At the Threshold of Brilliance:
The Brief but Splendid Career of Harold J. Rabinovitz

Cross-Country Chronicles:
Road Trips Through the Art and Soul ofAmerica

THE END OF THE BEGINNING

Jake

I should be grieving, crying a river, inconsolable. I'm the widower, after all, sole survivor of a conjugal train wreck, tragically alone at thirty-three.

"Poor Jake," they whisper as they gather at the gravesite. I spurned a service at her church, for reasons that will soon become evident, so this makeshift ceremony will have to suffice. Tucson's hotter than a habanero pepper and dry as a bone. Had it rained, I'd have appropriated a raindrop or two to stand in as tears.

"She was so young and beautiful! Thank God they didn't have children," they mutter as they await the brief rite from Benny, my buddy from Skip's Tavern. Okay, a guy I met last night at the bar. Told me from atop a barstool that he performed marriages. "Duly ordained and internet-trained," he boasted, in perfect poetic meter, "by the venereal Universal Life Church." Meant *venerable*, I suspect.

"Do funerals?" I asked him as he hunched over the bar, his bloodshot eyes barely visible over the foam of his Coors.

"Don't see why not," he said.

"Do my wife's and I'll cover your tab for a month."

"You're on," Benny slurred between belches. "What'll I say?"

"You'll figure it out."

Benny sets the record for burial brevity. "Kate Singer was a sweet, beautiful creature," he croaks, though he's never laid eyes on her. "And now she's dead," a line he inserts to erase any doubt. "May she rest in peace," he adds dutifully, like sprinkling dirt on the coffin. Seeking closure, he concludes with "Amen!" Had it occurred to me, I'd have engaged Benny's wife to sing something to give *me* closure—because it's not really over till the fat lady sings.

My equanimity perplexes the mourners as much as the pithiness of the proceedings. They watch me, befuddled, as I stand by the grave, dug by some tattoo-splattered gravedigger with nose rings like basketball hoops and ear lobes like Frisbees. I'm as stoic as the forest of headstones around me.

My eyes survey the gathering. Mom and Dad stand soberly beside me. I'm sure I detect an "I told you so" in Dad's pursed lips and furrowed brow. Mr. and Mrs. Olson, Kate's parents, flood their handkerchiefs with tears. Her three older brothers surround them like sentinels, glaring at me with disdain. Nick Davis, my law partner and best man at our wedding, heads the office contingent. They've come to pay their respects and win brownie points. Among them is the beautiful Christie Loring, in no need of brownie points, who casts furtive glances in my direction.

I've disappointed them all. They've offered support and I've responded with graceless indifference. I resolve to give them their due.

As the three-sentence service ends, they watch in bewilderment as I march through the aggregation of mourners. I advance aggressively toward a man my age whimpering behind a tree. He's thin and meek, dwarfed by my hulking frame. His black suit contrasts with his starched white clerical tab collar. I yearn to yank that presumptuous tab like the pop-top on a beer can, crushing his windpipe, but resist the temptation. Instead, an audible gasp arises from the assemblage as I cold-cock the sniveling clergyman with a left hook that would have impressed Ali. They scream as he collapses in a heap, blood pouring from his nose and mouth, imbuing that collar with the color of the desert sunset.

"*Holy shit!*" cries someone with a keen sense of irony.

THE BEGINNING OF THE END

Kate

My God, Jake! That's your wife in that box, not some pet hamster! I get that you're angry, but is that any way to say goodbye? No church service, just some bogus "minister" spewing bullshit while a man of the cloth cowers behind a tree till you beat him senseless in a disgraceful display of Neanderthal rage?

Then again, honey, I can't really blame you.

Poor Jake. Look what I've done to him. Give him an A for burial efficiency, but an F for mourning. I can't hold it against him. I've given him every reason to despise me. Heck, I didn't even make it home with the groceries I promised before leaving him.

So here I am, attending my own funeral. Most of us do—guest of honor, body shoved in a box—physically there, mentally absent. But I'm *consciously* present, seeing and hearing it unfold, as if I'd been sitting in the front row sucking in dust as they shoveled the sandy desert soil over that tacky wooden box.

And you know what bugs me even more than that creepy, seventeen-word send-off? That cow Christie Loring, all front and center, in that slinky black dress! Who dresses like that for a funeral? Had the hots for Jake since the day he hired her!

Poor Jake. Long nights at work with this hot, young thing with a thing for *his* thing. Jake never did own up to that. Innocent, he swore. And maybe he was. Curvaceous bimbo dabs at those crocodile tears with that hanky like she's plugging a leak, all the while making googly eyes at my poor, widowed husband. Crying my ass; she's ecstatic!

Good to see Mom and Dad, though. It's about time. First trip to Tucson—*ever*. I'd planned to surprise them with a visit, but that truck fucked it up. Pretty damn ironic, isn't it? Fertility doc told us to "keep on *trucking*"— because he couldn't say *fucking*. Well, the *fucking* ruined my life . . . and the *trucking* ended it.

I hadn't intended it, you understand. Idea kind of formed on its own, in the split second after I saw that bastard trucker hurtling toward me like a linebacker on steroids. Shifted that reusable bag of organic groceries from my right arm to my left, as if a bunch of oranges, a grapefruit, and a box of granola could cushion the force of the blow. But I can't take full responsibility—it wouldn't have happened if that yahoo hadn't been barreling down Sixth Avenue at just the right moment. Last thing I remember is the squeal of tires as my head smashed into the pavement like a pumpkin. Hit and run, they say. Gutsy play, just like in baseball.

So here I am, calling my own funeral like some cranky sportscaster. The ump rang me up, but I'm still at the plate. Invisible, but still freakin' here! How do I function? Where's my damn manual? Not online, I trust, because no one's coming to hook up the wi-fi.

Is this a detour on the journey to my final destination? Is there a purpose to my lingering presence? As to the first question, I'm as clueless as the body in that box. As to the second, I've got a notion.

PART ONE

In Order to Form
An Imperfect Union

CHAPTER ONE

Jake

We pushed through the heavy oak door of the Harvard Square Pub and ambled past the long wooden bar with its tarnished brass foot rail, beneath the peeling paint of its sagging beams. Harsh light from faux-Tiffany chandeliers exposed the cracks in its wood-paneled walls, like fissures in a dry creek bed. The pub was an anachronism, a once-grand saloon stubbornly persisting through its eightieth year, gamely putting its best face forward like an over-the-hill diva slathered with rouge. But the food was good, the service efficient, and the back-street location well insulated from the tourist-laden lunchtime crowds in nearby Harvard Square.

Jeremy, Mike, and I slithered onto the leather banquettes of our usual booth in the rear. A faded photo of the bar in its prime, bustling with men in homburgs, half-empty steins in one hand and smoldering cigars in the other, hung from the wall above us. The murmur of diners' voices mingled with the aroma of charbroiled burgers and the clatter of dishes and cutlery.

A little wisp of a girl in a starched white blouse and a short black skirt arrived to take our order. "I'm Kate," she announced buoyantly as she stood by the table, a notepad in one hand and a pencil in the other. "What can I get you?" With her boyish, short blond hair and dancing blue eyes, Kate was a far cry from the typical waitresses at the pub, weathered old biddies with harsh Boston accents addressing their patrons as "honey." They looked ludicrous in the skimpy waitress garb that Kate wore to such mesmerizing effect. Donning little or no make-up, she was unobtrusively beautiful, like the fresh-faced girl-next-door who'd blossomed while you weren't paying attention.

"God," I muttered to my colleagues in unconscious admiration, more audibly than intended.

"Not on the menu," she quipped. "St. Pauli Girl's as holy as we get." A mischievous grin flashed across her sparsely freckled face.

"Haven't seen you here before," Mike said.

"First day," Kate replied. "How am I doing so far?" Her accent was decidedly Midwestern.

"I'm awed," I said.

"So I gathered." Charming dimples bracketed an easy smile.

"I'm guessing you're not from around here," Mike surmised.

She shook her head coyly. "Unless this is Iowa."

As I fiddled with the menu, Mike and Jeremy ordered burgers, fries, and a Sam Adams, our brew of choice. Kate turned to me.

"How about you, holy man? What'll it be?" She brushed the tip of her pencil over the edge of her tongue in anticipation of my response.

"I'll have a burger, too."

"Two burgers."

"No, a burger *also*."

"Make up your mind, big guy. Fries with that?"

"Sure."

"Cole slaw?"

"Sure."

"A beer?"

"Sure."

"Sam Adams?"

"Sure."

"Rat poison?"

"Su—" Kate giggled as I caught myself. "On second thought, hold the poison."

"Thanks," she said with a wry smile before pirouetting and retracing her steps toward the kitchen.

Jeremy, Mike, and I stared shamelessly, watching her walk away, her little black skirt fluttering seductively with each graceful step.

The three of us were attorneys at Peabody & Green, the law firm I'd joined after graduation from Harvard Law School three years earlier. My tenure at the firm had already exceeded the duration of my star-crossed professional baseball career. Jeremy and Mike each had a wife, a toddler, and an unnaturally keen interest in the sex life of their unattached friend and colleague. They relished reliving their bachelor years vicariously through me. Jeremy began the assault the moment Kate disappeared from view.

"That's one hot piece of ass," he said, reverting, as was his habit in my presence, to his premarital vocabulary.

"So, Jake," Mike needled me, "why don't you ask her out?"

"She's not my type," I said, my eyes fixed on the menu.

"You mean she's not statuesque, pretentious, and bitchy?"

"A post-grad degree, an attitude, and a D-cup are Jake's threshold requirements," Jeremy alleged with a smirk.

Accustomed to these diatribes, I routinely ignored them. But nothing that day was routine. Maybe their relentless goading had finally taken its toll. Perhaps it was the kernel of truth in their observations about the women I dated. More likely, it was the inexplicable magnetism of this entrancing pixie of a girl. Blind to all reason, I took the plunge.

"Uh . . . Kate," I stammered at the end of our meal, fumbling with my napkin as she gathered our plates, "when do you get off tonight?" Trite. Clumsy. Like drilling a batter with a changeup on a two-strike count.

"What makes you think I'm *getting off* tonight?" she said with a puckish grin, balancing our dishes, glasses, and silverware with the dexterity of a juggler.

"I didn't mean—"

"Gee, now I'm disappointed," she grumbled, flashing a faux pout. My buddies found this hilarious.

"Let's try again," I said, both charmed and chastened. "Would you care to join me for dinner . . . after you've finished work?"

"Sure," she said without hesitation. "Why didn't you just ask?"

"Geez, Jake, we were just baiting you!" Mike said, shaking his head in disbelief as we departed the Pub. "I can't believe you actually asked her out!" His words triggered a jolt of high school déjà vu.

"You're old enough to be her father!" Jeremy added, unhelpfully.

Their reaction was understandable. I wasn't normally impulsive, especially with women—much less with women so young. I hadn't dated anyone Kate's age since college.

Although besieged by second thoughts in the hours that followed, I held fast. The brief sting of an ill-considered date would pale by comparison to the endless abuse I'd endure from Mike and Jeremy if I backed out now.

Kate and I met at the pub at the end of her shift. She'd swapped her waitressing getup for a tight pair of jeans and a red halter-top. I, on the other hand, was dressed like a sales clerk at Brooks Brothers. "Tee shirt and jeans in the wash?" she asked.

I'd reserved a table at one of the trendy restaurants for which Cambridge is known, but Kate demurred. "*Way* too fussy," she said, shaking her head in mock disapproval. "I've got a better idea." She snatched my hand and led me down Mass Avenue toward Central Square.

A few minutes later, we entered Antonio's, a nondescript pizza joint pinched between a bank and a travel agency near Central Square. The aroma of garlic, baking tomato, and bubbling mozzarella was seductive. Behind a glass counter, a swarthy, middle-aged man presided over a row of steaming pizzas. His dark red apron hung over his swollen abdomen like an awning. Unable to settle on a mutually agreeable combination of toppings, we ordered a half-and-half pie.

I grabbed a couple of beers from the cooler before it dawned on me that Kate was legally underage. A wave of guilt rippled through me as I imagined myself the wolf to her Little Red Riding Hood. Hoping she hadn't noticed, I exchanged them for Cokes.

"Reached your daily quota of Sam Adams?" she inquired.

"Uh . . ." I muttered.

"At least I'm not jail bait," she grinned.

We claimed a booth near the window. I felt strangely unmoored as I watched her settle in across the table. My impulsiveness at the pub that afternoon had both surprised and disturbed me. Except for her occupation, absurd youth (she'd claimed to be twenty, nine years my junior) and recent arrival from Iowa, I knew nothing about my dinner companion. Yet she intrigued me in a manner that defied explanation.

A tray arrived bearing our partitioned pizza, our tastes as divergent as our ages, apparel, and backgrounds. Kate's eyes gently shut as she inhaled the fragrance of the simmering pie.

"Mmmm," she sighed, devouring a slice swarming with artichoke hearts, zucchini, peppers, and a host of other nutritious toppings conspicuously absent from mine. "They don't make pizza like this in Iowa," she said.

Unqualified to comment on the quality of Iowan pizza, I asked Kate what had brought her to Cambridge.

"A bus," she replied, carefully extracting another slice from the tray. With her index finger, she delicately severed the gooey strands of mozzarella that clung to the adjacent slice.

"Fascinating," I opined. "Tell me more."

"Greyhound. Sixty seats. Air conditioning. Brakes groaned like a pig in heat." She punctuated the last sentence with a wink.

Her staccato responses amused me. "Are you trying to be funny or evasive?" I asked, inhaling a slice burdened with enough meat to make my arteries groan like her Greyhound bus.

"Yes," she said, smiling broadly, sighing almost orgiastically as she savored the pizza.

I guzzled my Coke, pondering my next inquiry. "Isn't Cambridge a bit of a culture shock?" I regretted the condescension inherent in my words as soon as they'd left my mouth.

Kate didn't flinch. "I cut off my pigtails, rinsed off the cow dung, and bought myself an iPad," she said between nibbles. "I'm even learning to drop my *r*'s."

Upon additional cross-examination, she acknowledged attending a small junior college in Cedar Rapids. "That, and a couple years of waitressing, barely qualified me for a job at the Pub," she acknowledged. Kate probed my background halfheartedly, as if to keep from revealing any more of her own. My legal and academic credentials intrigued her less than my baseball past.

"A righty, I presume," she said, glancing unabashedly at my left hand.

"Lefty," I corrected.

"Hmm..." she murmured, before broaching a subject my typical first dates were too genteel to address. "Jake," she asked, without a hint of embarrassment, "did you misplace your left index finger tonight?"

"A saga reserved for second dates," I replied, as we jointly inspected my four-fingered left hand.

After polishing off the last remnants of pizza, I invited Kate to my apartment for the proverbial nightcap. An impish grin conveyed her consent. While draining a bottle of merlot ("snooty, but satisfying," she declared, "with hints of chocolate, grapefruit, and bacon"), we watched the cult classic *The Little Shop of Horrors.* We drifted to the bedroom long before the movie ended.

Our lovemaking was ravenous. "Feed me!" she giggled, mimicking the commands of the movie's carnivorous plant. Kate, too, was no shrinking violet: she was self-confident and thoroughly at ease in her lithe, captivating body. A little tattoo of a five-petaled flower graced the delicate curve between her upper right buttock and the small of her back. "I think I found that missing finger," she beamed, convulsing with laughter as she observed my erection.

Kate's unpretentious disposition was a welcome departure from the intellectual presumption of my usual consorts. Unfettered by the baggage of urban sophistication, she was vivacious, spontaneous, and thoroughly charming. And Kate was more uninhibited than any woman I'd ever encountered—not what I might have expected from a farm girl swept suddenly into Cambridge like Dorothy into Emerald City. Her lone phobia seemed little more than a curious idiosyncrasy: she refused to make love with the lights on.

Kate commandeered my kitchen the next morning. With her small, pert breasts peeking out of the partially buttoned front of my Brooks Brothers shirt, she concocted a hearty Iowa country breakfast. Between forkfuls of hash browns and scrambled eggs, I asked if I could see her again that evening.

"On one condition," she said, savoring a crisp strip of bacon. "That you tell me the story behind that funky left hand."

"It's a deal," I confirmed, greedily attacking a plateful of buttermilk biscuits.

CHAPTER TWO

Kate

My parents owned a farm in Butte Rock, Iowa. As did their parents. And their parents' parents. Enough manure on those farms to fertilize all of Cambridge. Jake used to spout some quote from Sherlock or Oliver Wendell Holmes—I can't recall which—that went something like this: "three generations of imbeciles is enough." Well, that applies to farmers as well as imbeciles. I was damned if I'd be the fourth.

When I finished high school in '07, I fled to the big city—Cedar Rapids. Enrolled at Briscoe Junior College. Planned to squeak by on my earnings at Abe's Diner, a relic of the Fifties with wages and tips to match.

That's where I met Billy Garabedian. He waltzed into the diner for lunch one day in the spring of '09. Tall, pretty good-looking, but in a scruffy sort of way, half-shaved, with hair tied back into a fist-sized clump he proudly called his "man bun." Took a shine to me right off, checking me out like a thief casing a jewelry store. Came in every day for two weeks, making a beeline to one of my tables, chatting me up like a late-night TV host. Once, when all my tables were occupied, he sidled up to a couple of old ladies, offering to pay their tab if they'd scram. That ploy caught my attention.

Finally, he asked me out. I hesitated. A bit too slick, I

thought. But it was only a date, and he was nothing if not persistent. Like a fool, I accepted.

Billy took me to a noisy bar in the seedier part of Cedar Rapids—"Seedier Rapids," he called it. Ordered us a couple of burgers from the grill as we sat at the bar. I asked him what he did for a living.

"Make movies," he said, nonchalantly, as if he were some budding Steven Spielberg.

"What, in Cedar Rapids?"

"Yeah."

"What kind of movies?"

"Love stories."

"What, like *Casablanca*? *Sleepless in Seattle*?"

"Not exactly," he said. Before he could elaborate, our burgers arrived, and the conversation went elsewhere.

I didn't like the way he looked at me that night. Like a meat inspector examining a side of beef. Guys do that, of course, but Billy was obsessed, his eyes darting around every inch of my anatomy as we sat on those barstools. Figured he'd be all over me later that evening. But he ended it with an innocent little kiss. Strange, I thought.

Now don't get me wrong. Sure, I'm a country girl, but not the innocent blonde with pigtails you've conjured up in your imagination. I'll dispense with the false modesty: I've never had a problem attracting guys. Quite the contrary. In high school, the jocks tripped all over themselves chasing me, but they were no more appealing than the dumb-ass bulls strutting around the family farm: dim-witted, overfed piles of meat with a fondness for breeding. And it's not as if I didn't like sex—had my first encounter at thirteen, in fact. I spent my life on a farm, after all, with three older brothers and a barn full of randy animals. So, when some guy tells me he makes "love stories," well, I don't exactly blush. I'm not stupid enough to star in one, I figured, so if that's what he does for a living, it's fine with me, even if it is a bit sleazy. I'm not marrying this guy. Like they say in the song, girls just wanna have fun.

We dated a few more times. And Billy knew how to have fun. Knew the cool clubs in Seedier Rapids, the best bands, the top DJs. And sure, it wasn't long before he took me to his place—and it wasn't in Seedier Rapids, by the way, but in a higher-rent district. And yup, we got it on, and had as much fun in the sack as we did in the clubs. Probably more.

But the fling with Billy petered out quickly. Stopped coming into the diner, a no-show in the clubs. No big deal, I thought, there are plenty of fish in the sea.

In retrospect, I should've been more circumspect—if that's the right word. I didn't think it a big deal when Billy insisted we make love with the lights on. Said it aroused him. Well, he was certainly aroused, and so was I. But who knew there were cameras hidden in those bedroom walls? Billy did.

My girlfriend Louise pulled me aside after a class at Briscoe that May. "I hate to be the one to tell you this, Kate," she began, her eyes bulging like a couple of cow teats. You don't need a Harvard degree to guess the rest. "Your butt's on the internet," she told me, "and a whole lot more!" Everyone at school, except me, had seen it.

I cringe at my embarrassment when I finally gathered the courage to watch myself on the internet—for *twenty-seven fucking minutes*! It was humiliating! I imagined dirty old men wallowing in their erotic fantasies and pimply-faced teenage boys exploring their puberty, all while training their bug-eyes at me on their slimy little computer screens. It was *me* they were jerking off to. Me! Sure, I should've been suspicious about those bright lights—after all, I knew what the asshole did for a living. But it never occurred to me for a second that I was performing for an audience that night. Never dreamed he'd exploit me like that. I felt like an idiot. Afterwards, when men stared at me, I wondered if they recognized me. Did they worship me as a porn queen or revile me as something worse?

I made up my mind the next morning. Screw Cedar Rapids and Seedier Rapids! Screw Briscoe JC! Screw Abe's and, most of all, screw Billy Garabedian! I had to get as far away as possible. Didn't even hang around to graduate. I'd go where I could start out fresh, where no one knew me. New York was too big—it would swallow me up. I'd choose a college town—filled with people my age. Harvard was the best school I could think of. I gave my notice at Abe's, packed my bags, and boarded a Greyhound to Beantown.

CHAPTER THREE

Jake

I grew up in the Southern California city of Newport Beach, where Neiman Marcus nuzzles the Pacific.

My parents were overachievers. Dad obtained his undergraduate degree from Stanford and his law degree at Yale. He made a killing helping corporate raiders buy and dismantle asset-rich businesses, enriching everyone but the poor bozos who lost their jobs when the acquired companies were liquidated. Mom went to Cal-Berkeley and became a respected molecular biologist studying water flux across renal cortical membrane vesicles of carbonic-anhydrase-II-deficient mice. Really.

My parents were eternally busy: corporate raiders and carbonic-anhydrase-II-deficient mice are unduly demanding. I was the only kid they found time or inclination to beget. Absent a sibling, baseball was my constant companion.

I began pitching in Little League. I was bigger than my peers and threw harder. Much harder. I was the local, left-handed, Little League legend, blessed with devastating speed, but cursed with harrowing wildness.

When I was twelve, an angry pack of parents marched onto the field before my second game of the season. My first had been a qualified success: a no-hitter I'd won, 12-8. I'd fanned sixteen, walked eleven, and plunked four, all of whom were hauled from the field in tears.

No sooner had I taken the mound in that second game than the visitors' coach, accompanied by an *ad hoc* committee of distraught parents, confronted the umpire to demand my removal.

"He's gonna kill someone!" one parent contended, pointing to the ragged crew of Little Leaguers arrayed like tenpins along the top step of the visitors' dugout.

"No *fucking* way I expose my kid to this!" shrieked another.

Dumbfounded, I stood on the mound while the argument raged. But the umpire stood his ground, allowing me to remain in the game.

I faced my first batter when the mob dispersed. When my first pitch lodged in the batter's ribs, all hell broke loose. While the poor kid writhed on the ground, wailing in pain, the visitors' coach emptied his dugout, forfeiting the contest. Tears rolled down my cheeks as I stood by helplessly in witness to the carnage I'd wreaked.

Had Dad been there, he'd have threatened to sue the bastards for tortious interference with the emotional development of a minor. They'd have countersued, claiming assault with a deadly fastball.

To assuage the mutinous parents, Dad hired me a pitching tutor. I was too embarrassed to tell my friends, until I learned of their math tutors, science tutors, language tutors, ballet tutors, even tuba tutors. Everyone in Newport Beach had a tutor, trainer, mentor, or guru.

Under my tutor's tutelage, my command evolved. I became an unstoppable force, throwing four no-hitters in high school and reaching 94 miles-per-hour on the radar gun. By senior year, I had major league scouts drooling over me like pubescent teenage boys over a *Playboy* centerfold.

Constantly in the clutches of raiders and mice, my parents were largely oblivious. While Dad was quietly supportive of my athletic endeavors, he rarely saw me pitch. Mom couldn't tell a knuckleball from a knucklehead. It wouldn't have mattered if I'd been the second coming of Babe Ruth: in their eyes, athletic prowess took a back seat to academic achievement. It was hardly unexpected when they informed the groveling scouts that I was destined for college.

Despite our unambiguous message, the Cleveland Indians selected me in the 1997 amateur baseball draft, just weeks after my high school graduation. It was common for a team to take a late-round flyer on a draftee with college aspirations in hopes that fistfuls of money would trump academic resolve. The head of the Indians' scouting department flew out from Cleveland in a last-ditch effort to sign me before classes began at Stanford.

The head scout was Harley McGinniss, a former Indians' third baseman who'd signed his first pro contract right out of high school. He was bald, obese, and north of sixty, with eyebrows like hedgerows and teeth discolored from decades gnawing chewing tobacco. Harley arrived at our doorstep in a plaid shirt, worn khaki pants, and a faded Indians' cap. The suspenders he wore did more than support his pants: they precluded his collapse into a puddle of protoplasm. His mere appearance sabotaged his case before he could make it.

"What part of 'no' do you not understand?" Dad grilled him with his trademark, rapid-fire delivery, like the motor-mouthed radio announcer reciting commercial disclaimers.

"We'll give your son a scholarship," Harley promised, flashing his piano-keyboard smile, "advanced coaching . . . a chance to excel . . ." Dad rolled his eyes while I sat on the living room couch like a monk.

"I don't care if you give him the Rock and Roll Hall of Fame," Dad blustered, badgering the baseball relic with invective that would wither even the most hostile of courtroom witnesses. "He's getting a college education before he even *thinks* of pro ball. He's already *got* a scholarship to Stanford and, as you can see," he said, sweeping his left arm to showcase our affluence, "he's in no need of your Indian wampum."

"But—"

Dad ushered Harley out the door as if he were a religious proselytizer. With him went my first chance at a professional baseball career.

CHAPTER FOUR

Kate

I didn't expect to meet the man I'd marry on my first day at a new job in a strange city, just a week out of Iowa.

The Harvard Square Pub was just like its middle name: square. The waitresses were as old as my grandmother. When Jake asked me out—I knew, by the way, that his pushy friends had egged him on—I figured I had nothing to lose. I needed a friend and he was a good candidate. And handsome, in a buttoned-down way.

I'd never met anyone like Jake. Butte Rock has more stoplights (one) than Harvard grads. And I was as much a curiosity to him as he was to me.

Jake's buddies were as baffled as a rooster in a pigpen. A one-night stand, Mike and Jeremy figured, just a freaky fuck of a farmer's daughter. But, to their horror, we became a couple, and they'd just have to deal with it. Their disapproval was subtle, but unrelenting, like the burn of indigestion. I shudder to recall my one and only dinner with Mike and Jeremy—and their god-awful wives.

I was a nervous wreck as we drove to Jeremy's big new house in the suburbs. I knew I'd be out of my element.

"So, what's Jeremy's wife's name?" I asked Jake, prepping for the dreaded visit.

"Sue," he said.

"And Mike's?"

"Sue, too."

"Sue One and Sue Too?" Sounded like something out of Dr. Seuss. "Two *lawyers* with wives named Sue?"

"So nice to finally meet you, Kate," said Sue One with a smug little grin as the six of us sat in their living room. Spread before us was a tray of canapés, a snooty word she used to describe precious little Ritz Cracker wannabes lathered with something resembling pond scum. Short and dumpy, she looked like a tree stump in a pantsuit. Sue Too, big-snouted, round-faced and pale as an albino goat, resembled a prairie dog in a cocktail dress.

Jeremy and Mike had briefed their wives about Jake's underaged country bumpkin girlfriend. It was now up to the interrogation team of Sue & Sue—which sounded like an entry in a 4-H hog-calling contest—to make their husbands' demeaning label stick.

"That's a pretty dress, Kate," said Sue Too as I sank into the cushy beige sofa. Her smile was as fake as her crooked nose job. "Nordstrom's?"

"Goodwill," I said. It probably cost less than her pantyhose.

"What a clever place to shop for clothes!" Not only is she a country bumpkin, but a destitute one at that, a gold-digger milking Jake for all he's worth.

"Ah, that's right, you're a *waitress* . . . at the Harvard Square Pub," said Sue One, branding me as a penniless peon.

"And a damned good one!" Jeremy chimed in. His wife's dirty look wiped the smile off his face faster than a bull could mount a heifer.

"Don't they serve beer at the Pub?" Obnoxious question,

Sue One. It's a freaking pub, for God's sake. I nodded, averting my eyes from the canapés.

"And you're *old* enough to serve beer?" This was about Jake robbing the cradle.

"Yep," I said. "Just too young to drink it in public." I braced myself for the inevitable.

"How old *are* you, Kate?" asked Sue Too, reaching for her third helping of pond scum. Would she card me before serving the drinks?

"Sixteen." I said it with the sincerity of a nun.

Sue One was horrified. "My God, Jake!" She turned to him immediately, staring in disbelief. "Is she *serious*?"

"Of course not!" Jake howled, wondering, I suspect, if the Sues knew I was yanking their chains.

"Okay, well . . . *almost* sixteen," I chirped. "My birthday's next month, right Jakie?"

Jake was turning ashen. I couldn't tell if it was from the conversation or the canapés. "Jesus, people," he said. "She's twenty! Now leave the poor girl a—"

"Are you really from a place called *Butt* Rock?" asked Sue Too, twisting the pitchfork.

"That's Butte Rock," I replied, pronouncing it like *beaut.* "Ever been there?"

"Doubt it," she said. "Is it on the way to somewhere?"

"Emerald City," I said, "in the Land of Oz." Jeremy and Mike were giggling now, at their wives' expense, while Jake tried to maintain a straight face.

"I'm sure it's a wonderful place," Sue One said, patronizing me again.

"If you like corn," I countered. Mentioning corn reminded me I was getting hungry. You'd have thought they'd have served cheese or some other option to algae and crackers.

The interrogation continued. "Jeremy says you grew up on a *big ol'* farm." Sue One smirked, her lips puckered like a *big ol'* catfish.

"Don't worry, I wiped off the cow manure on your carpet on my way in," I assured her. "Maid can probably wash it out." Her smirk evaporated. "I'm joking," I said, but Sue One wasn't laughing.

But Mike and Jeremy *were* laughing, even harder now, and the more they laughed the angrier their wives became. "Okay, one last question," Mike said, a big grin on his face. "Where does one go for a good time in Butte Rock?"

"Under the bleachers," I said.

"Oh, my God!" cried a Sue (maybe two).

Jake, Jeremy, and Mike were nearly rolling on the floor. Neither of the Sues was the least bit amused.

With that comment, their fascination with the hick in their midst came to an end. For the rest of the evening, the Sues froze me out. The conversation turned to the symphony, international politics, law firm gossip, and the infantile competition among them for smaller and pricier electronic devices.

Dinner included pan-seared foie gras. I nearly gagged when I learned it was goose liver. Dessert was some unpronounceable soufflé. Sue One was petrified when it collapsed right out of the oven. Wailed as if her dog died.

Jake rescued me before I could embarrass us both by nodding off after dinner on their goose-down, designer sofa. What was it with Sue One and geese? I couldn't get out of the door fast enough.

"God, Jake," I said, nearly in tears. "They're so goddamn pompous!"

Jake could hardly debate my assessment. "I'm really sorry," he said, folding himself behind the steering wheel of our getaway car. "But you dished it back like a trouper." He fastened his seat belt, switched on the ignition, and stepped on the accelerator. "You were fabulous," he gushed, before noticing tears in my eyes. "You okay, Kate?"

This was the pivotal moment in our relationship, the point where logic should have triumphed over emotion. Jake and I had nothing in common. We both knew it. Our worlds mixed like oil and water. "What're we doing together, Jake?" I asked him, sniffling. I felt like Eliza in *Pygmalion*, a role I'd performed in a high school play. "If you think you can transform me from farmer's daughter to debutante," I said sharply, "you're barking up the wrong boar's ass!"

Jake burst out laughing. Pulled the car over, peered into my angry eyes, and smiled. Unbuckling his seat belt, he leaned over, placed his hands on my cheeks, and kissed me ever so deeply. "I love you exactly the way you are," he said. I melted; the anger drained from me like air from a blowout. It took a swine reference to extract his first declaration of love, but it was okay by me.

CHAPTER FIVE

Jake

I met Nick Davis on the first day of fall practice at Stanford. He was student manager of the baseball team, a little dork from Arizona with nary an athletic bone in his puny, underdeveloped body. As manager, Nick helped to coordinate practices, monitor and maintain equipment, organize travel, and—his favorite function—film and analyze practice and game action. Although we couldn't have been more different physically, we had two things in common: an interest in law—both of our fathers were successful attorneys and each of us harbored an expectation of ultimately following in their footsteps—and a rabid love of baseball.

Nick was the ultimate baseball junkie, with an unbridled passion for the National Pastime's history and statistics. He'd read biographies of all the baseball greats: from Ruth, Gehrig, Cobb, and Wagner to Williams, DiMaggio, Mantle, and Koufax; spouted statistics like a math savant; and scarfed down nuggets of baseball trivia like they were so many Cheerios in his breakfast bowl.

Nick wasn't some puppy dog sniffing around the jocks in the locker room. He was a brilliant student of the game. Adept at analyzing film, he diagnosed and helped me correct mechanical flaws in my pitching motion more times than I can count. He broke down advance film of opposition hitters to assess their strengths and weaknesses, assisting me in the preparation of game plans. Smart, funny, and self-deprecating, Nick Davis became—and remains—my closest friend.

Like those of most collegiate ball clubs, Stanford's schedule was dominated by a succession of three-game weekend series. The Friday night starter was the team's ace, Saturday's game was entrusted to the club's number two pitcher, and the third man in the rotation started on Sunday afternoon. I began freshman year as the Sunday starter, progressing one rung each year until junior year, when I inherited the mantle of Friday night ace.

With no small contribution from Nick, I was cruising through my junior year, sporting a nifty 7-1 record with an earned run average below two. Scouts hung around the ballpark every Friday night, training their radar guns on me like highway patrolmen with ticket quotas.

Junior year is key for college ballplayers with professional ambitions—it's the year they become eligible for the major league draft. I looked forward to the chance to turn pro, to have my shot at "The Show," the term we used to refer to Major League Baseball. While the best of my classmates would soon have their chances, mine vanished like a snowball in the desert.

It happened in Tucson, Nick's hometown, in March of 2000. I was coasting into the eighth inning against Arizona with a comfortable lead when I felt a twinge in my left elbow. Foolishly, I shouldered through the pain. Nick was the first to approach me when I returned to the bench at the end of the inning.

"Something happened out there," he said. There was genuine fear in his eyes. "You winced . . . and then you shifted your arm angle to ease the pain."

"I'm fine," I insisted with characteristic stubbornness. Nick saw through my subterfuge. When he motioned for the trainer, I knew it was the end of my day, my year, and quite possibly my career.

An MRI confirmed our worst suspicions: a torn ulnar collateral ligament in my left elbow. A month later, I underwent the dreaded elbow reconstructive procedure known throughout baseball as Tommy John surgery.

Touted as a sure first-rounder before the injury, my prospects plummeted. On the second day of the draft, Harley McGinniss called to report that the Indians had selected me in the twenty-fifth round. It was an underwhelming endorsement.

Recovery from Tommy John takes a year, at minimum. As a college junior, my choice was simple: sign with the Indians for a token bonus or complete my education and my final year of eligibility in hopes of reclaiming my premium draft status.

Doubling down on his unsuccessful attempt three years earlier, Harley made his second foray into Newport Beach, hoping to coax me to forgo my senior year and sign with the Tribe. It was a bold effort against insurmountable odds.

"What part of 'no' do you not understand *this* time?" Dad shrieked in lieu of a greeting when the grizzled old scout appeared at the front door unannounced on a Saturday morning in June. He looked like a door-to-door salesman in his garish plaid suit.

"All of it!" Harley shot back, his trademark suspenders flapping as violently as his vocal cords. McGinniss was emboldened this time. He waddled right up to Dad, screaming at him from point-blank range like an aggrieved manager verbally assaulting a haughty umpire. Though I was in earshot—as was the entire town—I was little more than an interested bystander as the scout and the lawyer butted heads for the second time in three years. "Your kid can finish school in the off-season," Harley insisted. "He'll have the fuckin' benefit of our crack medical and conditioning specialists to guide 'im through the rehab of his pitching elbow," he jawed. "Who are you to fuck up his dream?" A stream of tobacco juice dribbled from the lower left corner of Harley's mouth.

Nobody talked to Dad like that, not even the foul-mouthed Wall Street types he regularly devoured for breakfast. He was incensed. "I'm his father, goddammit!" Dad bellowed, burying his right index finger in the old scout's gut. "Like I told you the last time, you decrepit piece of shit, he'll finish his goddamn college education first," he blustered, showering Harley in a cloud of spittle. "Then he can play pro ball till he's eighty!"

"Fuck you, you motherfucking prick!" Harley shouted, slamming the front door behind him as he made his dramatic exit. Spitting out a few choice expletives, he stomped down the walkway, kicked in the driver's side of his rental car, and drove off.

Back at Stanford that fall, I embarked upon an extensive rehab program to maximize my chances of pitching in the spring. While the athletic trainers devised satanic exercise and stretching regimes, it was Nick who spent countless hours pushing and encouraging me. I was forbidden from throwing full-throttle until May, at which point only three weeks remained in the season. I could have chosen to sit it out, deferring my final year of eligibility to the following year, but it was time to get on with my life.

In May, I made my first mound appearance in a year,

throwing two perfect innings of relief. My elbow felt strong, and though my fastball was a tick under its previous velocity, my secondary pitches were sharp. I got into four more games before the end of the season, then pitched five effective innings of relief in a losing cause at the College World Series at Omaha. Though I'd thrown but a dozen innings in total, scouts saw that I was healthy again.

Harley McGinniss telephoned before the June draft. "If we choose you again, will you sign," he asked, "or will your Dad hold out for grad school and marriage?"

I laughed, apologized for my father's belligerence, and confirmed I was ready for pro ball.

"Great!" he said. "We're looking at selecting you somewhere between the sixth and ninth rounds."

But Harley was foiled again when the Boston Red Sox interceded, calling my name in round five. While I felt bad for Harley, Dad reveled in the old scout's misfortune. I promptly signed with the Sox and began my pursuit of The Show.

CHAPTER SIX

Kate

We'd been together nine months when Jake flew me to California to meet his parents. It was a big step, and I was petrified. If a dinner with his lawyer friends was awkward, imagine an entire weekend with his rich, ultra-educated parents. I knew little about them—only that his Dad was some high-powered lawyer and his Mom played with rats. What would they think of me? Or of their only son, a graduate of Stanford and Harvard Law School, shacking up with a waitress from Iowa? I knew they'd be sorely disappointed, and deep down, I think Jake knew it, too.

My first glimpse of California. I was in awe. And his parents' house was breathtaking. I'd gawked over homes in fancy magazines, but this was for real. More glass than the Boston Aquarium and better ocean views. I felt like a tourist on a celebrity house tour.

Jake had warned me about his Dad. Called him "formidable."

"What's that mean, Einstein?" It was a nickname his baseball buddies had foisted on him years ago. He didn't much care for it; got it because he'd be reading Tolstoy or Hemingway while they were thumbing through comic books and playing video games.

"You'll see," he said, so I braced for the worst.

But it was better than I'd imagined. Phil, Jake's Dad, was

loud and opinionated, but he was charming as well, like Jake. Bragged a bit about screwing some idiot business types who seemed to have it coming, but toned it down when Jake's mother gave him a blistering look. Maybe *she* was the formidable one. Julia Singer was really sweet. Did everything possible to make me comfortable, and that was no small task.

"Hope you remembered your bathing suits," Julia said as she led us over the massive redwood deck to their spectacular pool. Jake had insisted I bring a bikini he worshipped. I was hesitant: it consisted of less fabric than an eyepatch. He persisted. I think he wanted to impress his Dad. "Why don't you change," Julia suggested, "and take a dip before dinner."

"Cocktails poolside in thirty!" Phil announced.

"Where are the rats?" I asked Julia, as we sat on elegant deck chairs arranged in a cluster beside the pool, its blue water rippling in the soft ocean breeze. Phil plied us with margaritas the size of birdbaths.

Julia laughed. "I give them the weekends off," she said. I must have looked puzzled.

"They're in a lab about five miles away," Jake explained with a smile.

"Oh," I said, before nearly gagging on my mind-numbing drink.

"Amazing, aren't they," Phil said. I couldn't tell whether he was referring to his margaritas or to the breasts peeking out from the shards of fabric he'd been unsuccessfully trying to ignore.

"Certainly are," Jake said, smirking. I stifled a grin.

As he dove into his second margarita, Phil asked me about life in Iowa. Given my lack of academic or professional accomplishments, it was the only topic remaining for discussion. But I'll grant them this: Jake's parents were gracious and never condescending, unlike the pompous Sues. So, I told them all about life on a farm. In fact, I related my whole life story—it doesn't take long—except for the part about being a porn star. Hadn't even shared that with Jake . . . and didn't plan to.

CHAPTER SEVEN

Jake

A week after signing with the Sox, I found myself with the Lowell Spinners, a Single-A farm club whose uninspiring logo featured a skein of yarn twisted like a noose around the barrel of a choking bat. But I was one of the lucky ones. While many of my college teammates started their pro careers in crumbling old ballparks in God-forsaken cities in Appalachia or the upper Midwest, I played in a new park amid renovated mills and dormant smokestacks strung along the Merrimack River less than an hour from Fenway Park.

My roommate at Lowell was Fuckin' Danny Boyer, an undrafted infielder from a junior college in the heart of West Texas. A half-foot shorter and sixty pounds lighter than I, he earned his nickname by using it in nearly every sentence he uttered. Danny and I had nothing in common. While I read novels, Danny devoured comic books. I watched *West Wing*; Danny favored *Survivor.* I listened to jazz; Danny inhaled country music. He viewed me with a mixture of incomprehension and disdain, as if I were some exotic beast.

But on the diamond, Danny was the beast. He overcompensated for his limited physical attributes by playing harder than everyone else. In his mind, there was nothing he couldn't do as well as the more highly touted prospects on the roster, and he was constantly committed to proving it.

My first professional start came in mid-June of 2001. We were playing at home, against the Mahoning Valley Scrappers, the Indians' farm team for which I'd be playing if Harley McGinnis had had his way. The same Harley McGinnis who suddenly materialized like an overinflated parade float along the right field foul line as I completed my pre-game warm-ups.

"Hey, kid," he chortled, his ill-fitting uniform straining to contain his ever-increasing girth. "Break a leg!" Though Dad might have interpreted it differently, I took it as the magnanimous gesture it was, particularly in light of the abuse he'd absorbed from my father. On a scouting assignment, Harley was evaluating the talent the Indians had selected in my stead. "I pushed hard to move you up on the draft board," he swore, "but the brass wouldn't cooperate. I've got a gut feeling you're gonna prove 'em wrong."

"Thanks, Mr. McGinniss," I said, dodging the tobacco-laden slobber descending from his lips like sludge from a leaky drainpipe. "At least you didn't have to negotiate my contract with Dad."

"I was hit in the head three times during my playing days," he muttered as he leaned forward unsteadily, his hands firmly entrenched in his back pockets. "None was any tougher than sparring with your father." He let out a guffaw, more equine than human. "But each time you go down in this life, you get up, dust yourself off, and get back in the box. That's what it's all about, son." He spit out advice as liberally as tobacco juice, but it was advice worth remembering.

The game was scoreless when I left the mound after the fifth inning. I'd thrown seventy-three pitches, two shy of my limit, so I was done for the evening. I'd allowed three singles, struck out seven, and walked one—a good debut by any measure. But it was Danny who handed me the victory that night. In the bottom of the fifth, he laid down a perfect bunt, beating it out for a hit; stole second and third on successive pitches; and scored on a close play at home after tagging up on a short fly to right. The margin held, as we beat the Scrappers, 1-0.

Danny and I celebrated with a couple of six-packs of Sam Adams. What he lacked in size he made up for in capacity, pounding down two brews for each I consumed. As the night wore on, his tough-guy façade eroded.

"I'm fuckin' homesick," he grumbled. "Fuckin' hate New England! Fuckin' cold at night even in fuckin' June," Danny moaned, finishing off another fuckin' Sam Adams. "I miss my buddies; my girlfriend, Angela; even the sweet fuckin' smell of Texas crude." He described in excruciating detail the various ways in which he'd prefer to be fuckin' Angela at that very moment, rather than suckin' down beers named for patriots with some "fuckin' Einstein" from "Stamford," even though, he allowed, "you throw one fuckin' awesome heater." It wasn't articulate, perhaps, but it was, on some level, a welcome expression of acceptance and respect.

Danny's defensive prowess saved my ass on more than one occasion that summer. And by the time it was over, I found myself listening contentedly to the country music of Garth Brooks, Kenny Chesney, and Tim McGraw on Danny's fuckin' boom box. For his part, Danny actually managed to read a novel I'd recommended: J.D. Salinger's *The Catcher in the Rye.* While he felt somewhat deceived—he thought it was about baseball—he admitted it had intrigued him. Both of us were pleased with our on-field accomplishments as well. Danny hit a robust .320 and I finished the season with a 5-1 record and a sparkling 2.45 earned run average. My elbow held up and my velocity increased as the summer progressed. It was a good year—and my last hurrah.

CHAPTER EIGHT

Kate

Turns out that darling Jake had something up his sleeve when he took me to meet the Singers of Newport Beach: the M-word. It's not that I was opposed to the idea. I was rather fond of the nine-fingered lug, and we were head over heels in love. But love made us no less of a mismatch: farm girl/waitress/porn star (he still didn't know that part) and Einstein/lawyer/athlete. We should've known better.

Jake proposed to me on May 10, 2010. It was my twenty-first birthday. He'd cradled the ring in the sweat-stained pocket of his old baseball glove, stuffing them both in a cardboard box covered with birthday wrapping paper.

"You're giving me your greasy, old baseball glove?" I said, underwhelmed, as I opened the package. "Jesus, Jake."

"Put it on," he insisted.

"Come on," I groused, "I'm not even left-handed!" I humored him. When I maneuvered the smelly old thing onto my right hand, the ring spilled out, clanking onto the floor. It was beautiful. Eighteen-carat white gold, a big diamond in the center flanked by five petals, each filled with clusters of smaller diamonds. Reminded him, he said, of that flower tattoo near my butt. "Fuck, yeah!" I giggled, lunging into his arms. And then we made love—with the lights blaring.

We were married four months later at the Immanuel Lutheran Church in Butte Rock, Iowa. It was on the ninth anniversary of 9-11. We were probably tempting fate.

Only fifty people attended—it was hardly a destination wedding. On my side, it was mostly family: my three brothers—that fourth generation of farmer-imbeciles—along with a host of cousins, grandparents, aunts, and uncles. My girlfriend Louise served as my bridesmaid. "One peep about that porno and I'll slaughter you with my bare hands," I'd warned her.

My parents met their future son-in-law three days earlier. It was like introducing an Angus to a herd of Holstein. While impressed by his charm, his looks, and his resume, they couldn't fathom the gulf in our backgrounds. Jake's friends, I'm sure, felt the same way.

Jake's parents arrived the day before the wedding. I can only imagine what went through their minds as they rattled down the dusty, half-mile road, past endless rows of five-foot cornstalks, teeming hog pens, and a big, old barn, before pulling up in front of the rambling farmhouse built by Great Grandpa Olson on the eve of the Depression. It was a far cry from their palatial glass mansion overlooking the Pacific. Formidable Phil wore a black power suit with a bright red tie while Julia looked California chic in a neatly tailored pantsuit. The looks on their faces were precious as they politely shook hands with my overall-clad father and my mother in her frumpy housedress.

After the awkward introductions, I took Phil and Julia to their room in the rear of the house. Though hardly the Ritz, Julia declared it "charming." I offered to show them around the farm, suggesting they change into something more suitable for hurdling mud puddles and dodging cow pies. They emerged from their room ten minutes later, ratcheted down to business casual. They'd forgotten, evidently, to pack their mud boots and overalls.

Jake's parents endured their tour with grace. Phil was politely curious about the farm's operations: its crops, machinery, and livestock. The sight of a boar mounting a sow prompted a smirk from Phil and a slightly astonished "Oh, my!" from Julia.

After the tour, the families of the bride and groom convened in the dining room for the rehearsal dinner—an old-fashioned country feast. It felt like the Pilgrims and Indians at the first Thanksgiving.

Though blissfully ignorant of rural etiquette (or lack thereof), Jake's parents handled their Middle American encounter with remarkable poise. And if they'd failed to endorse Jake's choice of a bride, they never revealed their displeasure.

Dinner, of course, was a fiasco. Who knew that neither Phil nor Julia were meat-eaters? Jake certainly ate meat: that was obvious from his first slice of pizza at Antonio's. In Newport Beach, we'd been served only fish, salads, and meatless pastas, I realized in retrospect, but I'd drawn no conclusions from the menu selections. It was awkward when Dad proudly unveiled a massive porterhouse steak.

"Um," Jake whispered in my ear. "Mom and Dad don't eat meat."

"Oh, shit," I said.

"Something wrong?" my mother asked.

"Phil and Julia don't eat meat," I said.

"How is that possible?" asked my father.

"It's healthier," Phil replied.

Dad erupted. "Nothing unhealthy 'bout this animal!" he

exclaimed. "Slaughtered 'im myself!" Julia turned green. "Darn it, Kate, why didn't you tell me?"

"Sorry, Dad, I didn't realize."

"Honey, maybe you can whip up somethin' that doesn't *bleed*," Dad said to Mom while the rest of us cringed.

"No, no," Julia insisted. "We're fine. That fresh-picked corn looks luscious." Phil and my father sighed in unison.

The wedding meal was a whole roasted pig.

CHAPTER NINE

Jake

We've reached the point in the story you've all been waiting for: the saga of the missing digit, the story that secured my second date with Kate. I've told it more times than I can tick off (that means more than nine), and it stings like hell each time I tell it.

On the strength of my performance at Lowell, I broke spring training camp in 2002 with the Trenton Thunder of the Eastern League. A Double-A franchise, Trenton was just a couple of rungs from The Show.

Though within hailing distance of Philadelphia and New York, Trenton made Lowell feel like Newport Beach. The team nickname, Thunder, was a more marketable version of the local soundtrack: gunfire. With a rate of violent crime nearly four times the national average, Trenton was a patch of toxic weeds in the midst of the Garden State.

Our ballpark was an oasis in a sea of urban deterioration, a mere half-mile stroll—or more advisedly, gallop—from the New Jersey State Prison, a maximum-security prison in the heart of the city where the state's death row inmates resided.

I lived with two teammates in a small, three-bedroom house we rented a few miles from Trenton's ghetto. With life in the minor leagues so transient, roommates came and went like colds. Heath Renfro, a right-handed pitcher from the University of Florida, lasted just two weeks. He was bombed in his first two starts and took issue with our old-school manager, Whitey Wilcox, when Whitey strolled to the mound to remove him from his second outing. Despite an earned run average higher than the crime rate, Heath made the mistake of calling Whitey a motherfucker—the baseball equivalent of the N-word—while showing up his manager by openly resisting his removal from the game. By the next morning, Heath had been dispatched to the rookie league, two rungs down the organizational ladder, a demotion he appreciated even less than his early hook the night before.

I met our new roommate, Ricky "the Flash" Ryerson, the next day. We'd all heard the name. He was that year's phenom, a first-round draft selection from some podunk high school in the Oklahoma Panhandle who'd signed with the Sox for a cool couple million. He had a 98-mile-an-hour heater and a curve as crooked as a prizefighter's nose. He was a six-foot-four-inch hulk with a head as swollen as his wallet. While the Sox wouldn't ordinarily promote a kid so young this quickly, he'd been so dominant at the lower levels that it made sense to challenge him further. If only his maturity had caught up with his seven-figure bonus.

The Flash—he insisted we address him that way—drove up to our house in a shimmering silver-gray Porsche Carrera. I directed him to Heath's old room, the smallest in the house.

"The Flash is preturbed," he complained, butchering the language while steadfastly referring to himself in the third person. "Room's the size of a fuckin' closet," he said, depositing his neon-hued Nike gym bags on the floor. "Yours bigger?" he asked me.

"Yup."

He reached for his wallet and peeled off a hundred-dollar bill. "Trade ya," he said, as if he were some ten-year-old bargaining with his kid brother.

"Nah, I'm good where I am," I said.

"Well fuck you, then." He was seething as I left the room. Our other roommate was less principled and took the cash.

Emboldened by his earlier success, The Flash figured that all he needed to do to excel at Double-A was to show up, that his God-given talent would ensure success. He wasn't the first phenom to flame out and won't be the last. Wild in his first start, he lasted only two innings before Whitey gave him the hook.

The Flash pouted after his inauspicious debut, blaming the weather, the umpiring, his catcher, and the topography of the mound for his meltdown. He slept late, shirked workouts, and ignored his teammates, all of whom dismissed him as a spoiled jackass. He frittered away his bonus as if it were Monopoly money, buying thousand-dollar suits, $400 shoes, and a $10,000 sound system that repeatedly fried our fuses. Eschewing electricity was preferable to enduring the infernal pounding of his subwoofers.

But the real problems developed ninety miles from Trenton, in the casinos of Atlantic City. Instead of returning to the house after night games, The Flash would hop into his Porsche and head for the Boardwalk. When he grew tired of the crap tables, he took to poker, graduating from the public low-stakes games to the backroom tables frequented by professional gamblers. He stayed out all night. When he'd whittled his bonus down to a nub, he borrowed, at rates even higher than his ever-inflating earned run average, from men with names like Shorty and Guido.

Burning the candle at both ends soon earned The Flash a return ticket to the lower minors. We had one of our few conversations in his room on the day of his demotion.

"Tough break, Ricky," I said, refusing to address him by his self-appointed nickname.

"No problem," he said, quickly stuffing his belongings into his deluxe gym bags. Given his ego, I expected a tirade of blame and excuses. Instead, he seemed eager to leave.

"Wanna talk about it?" I asked.

"Nope," he said. He zipped up the last bag and rose to leave. He'd made no effort to collect the untold thousands in electronic equipment scattered about his room.

"Uh . . . Ricky. . . aren't you forgetting something?" I motioned at the tower of sleek audio equipment arrayed across the room like a city skyline.

"It's yours," he said, dragging his gym bags out the door, down the stairs, and into the back seat of his convertible. Within seconds, the screech of his Michelin tires and the smell of burning rubber verified his departure.

The Flash, as it turned out, left me more than his sound equipment. He left me the consequences of his gambling debts, a fact that became apparent two hours later when a white Hummer with Jersey plates pulled into the driveway while I sat on the front porch plodding through a giant tome by Tom Wolfe. As luck would have it, my other roommate was away that afternoon.

Two burly men exited the tank-like vehicle and sauntered up the porch steps. They were clad in wrinkled black suits and sunglasses like the Blues Brothers and each carried a battered Louisville Slugger in his right hand.

"Inside, Ricky" the first one ordered. Pot-bellied and

double-chinned, he looked and sounded like a goon from the Sopranos. The second, taller and less rotund, was a doppelganger for Elwood, Dan Aykroyd's character in the Blues Brothers movies. Of course, I immediately informed them that I wasn't Ricky. Ricky and I were of similar size and build, but I was at least five years older than The Flash. Neither was persuaded by my declaration.

"Shut up and step inside," Elwood demanded. He grabbed me by the collar and dragged me inside the front door, the bat cocked above his shoulder like a Neanderthal's club.

I briefly entertained the notion that this was all an elaborate prank. Minor leaguers, blessed with an abundance of free time, were masters of the practical joke, and the baseball bats seemed a dead giveaway. But when Pot-Belly slammed his fist into my jaw, I quickly dismissed that hypothesis and adopted a mantle of genuine fear.

"You've got the wrong—" Another blow to the face.

"You had your chance, Ricky," Elwood said. "Open your mouth again," he threatened, brandishing his Louisville Slugger, "and you'll be sucking down meals with a straw."

I figured this was Ricky's warning, that I'd already endured the worst. But when Pot-Belly extracted a bolt cutter from his jacket pocket, I panicked and broke for the door. Elwood hit me like a linebacker, knocking me to the floor. Pot-Belly pounced on my chest, straddling it, while Elwood grabbed my left hand and brutally spread my fingers, like he was snapping a wishbone.

The next few seconds are etched in my mind like a cattle brand. Pot-Belly grasped the bolt cutter, bent down, and snipped my index finger just below the knuckle, as if he were a landscaper trimming an overgrown shrub. I screamed like a teenage girl in a grade-B horror movie. Blood spurted from my stump like steam from an overheated car radiator. I had all I could do to keep from passing out.

"Next time, Ricky, it'll be your pitching hand!" Pot-Belly snickered, wiping the bolt cutter on my shirtsleeve and returning it to his jacket pocket. If only I'd been right-handed—like The Flash.

"PRO CAREER CLIPPED BY CASE OF MISTAKEN IDENTITY" proclaimed a headline on the front page of *The Trenton Times*. "THUGS CUT SHORT PROMISING PITCHING CAREER" graced page one of *The Trentonian*. It was probably the first time in decades that a maiming, rather than a murder, had captured the local headlines in New Jersey's violent capital city. The Red Sox were so outraged that they moved their Double-A franchise from Trenton after the 2002 season. Dad, of course, threatened to sue. "They'll cut off *your* finger," I warned him, "or maybe my balls, so don't even think about it." I was so outraged that I applied to law school. My baseball career was over.

I'm not sure what's worse: having your index finger forcibly amputated by a mob goon or spending three years at Harvard Law School. A monument to professorial arrogance and cutthroat competition, I felt lucky to emerge with my other nine digits intact. After serving my time, I parlayed my Harvard Law degree into a job at Peabody Green in Cambridge, and the rest, as they say, is history.

CHAPTER TEN

Kate

I endured one New England winter before our marriage. Swore it would be my last. Brutal. Pretty when it falls, the snow turns blacker each day, as if sprinkled by a shaker of coal dust. Sidewalks coat with ice, making every step an adventure. Then there's the "T," Boston's ancient transportation system, which seizes up with the first snowflake like a tractor caught on a stump.

It was at our wedding reception that Nick Davis, Jake's college buddy and best man, let slip that he'd been recruiting Jake to join his family law firm in Tucson. "Been trying to entice him for three years," Nick told me, "but haven't made any headway. He's a stubborn guy, your new husband," he said, not telling me anything I didn't already know. "Maybe you can talk him into a visit. Come in December," he laughed, "when Cambridge feels like Siberia."

So I badgered Jake for the next three months.

"I've never been to the desert," I'd say.

"It's hot, it's dusty, and I blew out my elbow there," he'd counter.

I'd pout, then turn up the thermostat. "It's cold here," I'd complain.

"It's fifty degrees outside."

"It's eighty in Tucson."

"You never take me anywhere."

"We haven't even been married two months! Where do you want to go?"

"How about Tucson?"

A week later, as the temperatures plummeted, Jake finally relented, agreeing to an early December getaway to Tucson. We barely escaped Logan Airport, as the winter's first snowstorm pummeled Boston. Perfect!

Nick and his wife, Trudy, a local real estate agent, were gracious hosts. While Nick courted Jake at his downtown law office, Trudy took me hiking in Sabino Canyon, chauffeured me through Saguaro National Park, and wooed me with the unexpected winter wonderland of Mt. Lemmon, where the snow was pure white. She even snuck me into a few of her property listings, proving how much more cheaply one could live in Tucson than in Cambridge.

The Southwestern desert was everything I'd imagined, and more. Mountains glowing red in the sunset, gnarly saguaro cactuses springing from the foothills like a child's stick-figure drawings. The skies were blue. The weather was pleasantly warm by day and refreshingly cool at night. The broad, wide-open roads offered stark contrast to the choking congestion of Cambridge. I thought of the filthy snow banks that would greet us upon our return to New England and knew that my days there were numbered.

Jake met the lawyers in Nick's firm. Nick's father, who'd founded the firm thirty years earlier, was ready to retire, and Nick wanted someone to take over his Dad's corporate practice. With his business and high-tech background, Jake was ideal. Nick and his colleagues pursued him like coyotes chasing a jackrabbit. They wasted no time, offering a full partnership.

"Dad can ride off happily into the sunset knowing you'll capably attend to his corporate clients," Nick told us at dinner on the second night of our visit. "And your seventy-hour work week will become a distant memory."

"I'd be making less than half of what I make now," Jake warned me later that evening as we readied for bed.

"Who cares?" I told him, reminding him that we'd have more time to spend together. "And we can live like royals here for what it would cost to buy a hovel in Cambridge."

"It's a hundred degrees here all summer," he noted. "You can cook eggs on the pavement."

"We'll get a house with a stove so I won't have to," I told him. "Better yet, we'll turn on the air conditioning."

"They've got rattlers, bobcats, and Gila monsters."

"They'll make wonderful pets," I said. "Our kids will adore them."

His defenses melted in the desert sun.

CHAPTER ELEVEN

Jake

I never told Kate about the conversation with my father. It took place on our visit to Newport Beach, in the kitchen on Sunday morning. Kate had been upstairs dressing.

"She's pretty and vivacious, I'll grant you that," Dad began, sitting at the kitchen counter sipping a cup of premium, custom-ground coffee "harvested lovingly," the label alleged, "from the rich volcanic soils of the lower slopes of Mount Kilimanjaro." I braced for the damning conjunctive clause. "But she's just a kid," he said, "and hardly your intellectual peer."

I opened the cabinet, grabbed a tumbler, and poured myself some tap water harvested lovingly from the Orange County Water District. "Sometimes you just want to be happy," I said.

"Hmmm," he muttered, returning the cup to his lips.

"I'm going to ask her to marry me, Dad."

He exhaled deeply. "Are you sure, Jake?" His disapproving tone was tempered by the quality of his "uniquely singular" coffee-drinking experience.

"I'm sure, Dad."

"I give it two years, three at the most." Rather prescient, as it turned out, but for reasons neither of us would have imagined.

"I didn't request your assessment," I said. Dad's opinions were rarely requested, but perpetually forthcoming.

"You're making a mistake, son," he said, looking me straight in the eye.

"It's my mistake to make, Dad, isn't it?"

It was, and I made it.

Kate and I began our lives in the desert in a rented condominium perched on the west side of the Catalina Mountains, just north of the city. While I settled into my practice at the newly denominated Davis, Davis & Singer, Kate scoured the city with Trudy in search of a more permanent abode.

Kate fell in love with a boxy, classic mid-century modern house in the historic Sam Hughes district. Close to the University of Arizona and my downtown office, the house was built of concrete block with a low-sloped roof, vaulted ceilings, wood floors, clerestory windows, and a nice little backyard in-ground pool. It also had leaky pipes and served as a termite convention center. None of that deterred Kate, who was dogged in her campaign to acquire the eventual money pit. It wasn't the first evidence I'd seen of Kate's single-minded determination. Nor the last.

What our new house lacked was something that money couldn't buy: kids. Kate couldn't wait to have kids. It soon became her primary objective. The prospect of settling down first and working a few years to amass financial security held little appeal to her. I, too, wanted kids, but was in less of a hurry. There was plenty of time, I thought.

"Why should I waste my best child-bearing years dishing out burgers and omelets when I can nurture our little ones, teach them to walk, talk, and swim? I want adorable little Jakes and Kates running circles around us, laughing and smiling," she said. She aimed to produce a herd of rambunctious shin kickers and wanted to start quickly to maximize the yield. We'd talked about children before, of course, but in more conventional quantities.

We came to an understanding. We'd try for a child right away, but Kate would wait tables until the late stages of pregnancy. And we'd forgo the assembly line for a more deliberate approach.

We discarded all birth control and let nature take its course. Unfortunately, nature was in less of a hurry than Kate. After a year, she dragged me to a fertility clinic. While Kate was having her equipment surveyed by beady-eyed perverts in white lab coats, I was jerking off into a plastic cup to the accompaniment of insipid porno videos like *Forrest Hump* and *On Golden Blonde*. "Stick it in there, big boy!" instructed the impossibly buxom "actress." Although my ejaculate was judged to display "below normal motility" (i.e., the little spermfuckers were a gaggle of slackers), Kate ovulated like a bitch in heat. The "fertility specialist" gave me a low-dose prescription of some concoction as a consolation prize, while urging us to "just keep on trucking" as he giggled inanely through his Ernest Hemingway beard.

So Kate and I kept on "trucking." Day after trucking day, night after trucking night, until we couldn't truck anymore. Another six months passed without a bun in the oven. Kate turned desperate. Thermometers, carefully scheduled liaisons, and warm scrotal compresses dominated our First Stage of Propagation Desperation.

I came home from work one day to find my underwear smoldering in the fireplace. "What the fuck, Kate?" I shouted.

"Tight underwear can impede fertility," she explained, citing her hairdresser's girlfriend's sister as the source of such wisdom. "I bought you a big box of bigger boxers," she announced, curiously pleased with herself. The boxers were four sizes larger than what I'd worn for the last fifteen years. When I reluctantly tried one on, my penis felt like a comma in a four-page run-on sentence.

Then there was the Kate Singer Fertility Diet. I was at the mercy of Kate, the Diet Patrolwoman. Fruits and vegetables had to be organic. Red meat was taboo. No more burgers and fries. What meat we ate had to be raised and slaughtered in splendor. We could only eat pork from hogs raised in commodious pens lined with clay diluted with Perrier. Chickens and turkeys were guaranteed a hedonistic lifestyle on idyllic farms run by the old farmer from *American Gothic* and the wife, daughter, or barnyard bimbo beside him with that funny look in her eyes, like she was fucking tired of his use of the pitchfork as a sex toy. We could only consume fowl raised in climate-controlled condominiums with top-shelf multi-speaker sound systems, room to exercise, Pilates classes, therapists, and copies of *Fifty Shades of Grey* translated into cock-a-doodle-dooish. Our pampered poultry had to be antibiotic-free, relegated to a life of wheezing and coughing, teeming with chicken pox or other frightful fowl afflictions, before being read their last rites, moments prior to slaughter, by a rotating cadre of ministers, priests, and rabbis dressed in chicken suits. And slaughter would have to be humane, an oxymoron if ever there was one: a quart of single malt scotch would have to be administered to render the mollycoddled little chickadees insensitive to pain before termination using a Second Amendment-certified concealed weapon so the poor bird wouldn't see it coming (assuming, of course, that all legal appeals had first been exhausted). No wonder we paid so much for food!

Next came the Sir Isaac Newton Stage of Propagation

Desperation, when Kate decided that gravity was the answer. It began with a modified "bicycle" exercise after sex: no sooner would I climax than she'd lift her hips into the air and mimic cycling, "to let those little fuckers work their way up to Egg City," she claimed. The next phase of the Newton Stage was characterized by a sexual position she called "inverted sex" (which I dubbed "perverted sex"). She demanded that I enter her standing up, with her virtually upside down resting on her shoulders. I felt like an aerial dive-bomber shooting tracers into a forest.

The third, or Internet Stage of Propagation Desperation, was even more bizarre, informed by an irrationality more pervasive than the old wives' tales of the Dark Ages. This stage was characterized by home remedies Kate gleaned like a bag lady from obscure corners of the internet. First, she guzzled cough syrup, convinced that the expectorant that thins the mucous in the lungs would have a similar effect on her cervical fluid, making it easier for my candy-ass sperm to swim through the muck and reach her egg. Nothing changed, though Kate didn't cough for months. Then came "fertility yoga." According to a website, "fertility yoga uses specific body poses, breathing techniques and guided imagery" in order to "strengthen, align, and properly position" the reproductive organs and support the "hormonal feedback loop" to enhance fertility. For weeks, I watched as she contorted herself into increasingly awkward positions while "visualizing" herself six months pregnant. Realigned and still not pregnant, she eschewed intercourse entirely, instead administering hand jobs for the purpose of harvesting a load of guppies that she would then inject like a mad scientist into her hungry vagina using an ordinary turkey baster that would hopefully never again see Thanksgiving. I felt like a bull on a dairy farm.

When all else failed, we resorted to in vitro fertilization. We endured two cycles without success. By this time Kate was a lunatic whose all-consuming desire to achieve pregnancy had put not just our sex life, but our entire marriage, in jeopardy. In time, I found sex with Kate so demeaning and bizarre that I could no longer even manage an erection. Kate took it personally. That sweet country girl had turned into a monster, berating me at every opportunity, blaming me for all of our failures. Her pet words for my penis were "slack jack," "brick dick," and "mock cock."

Finally, in utter desperation, Kate turned to religion. It was the straw that broke this camel's back.

CHAPTER TWELVE

Kate

I make no apologies. I wanted kids, lots of kids. I wanted them now; Jake wanted them later. But, as Jake will attest, I *can* be persistent.

I couldn't spend all my time screwing and peeing on a stick in hopes of the desired indication, so I took a job at Mel's, a little diner wedged into a bland strip mall on the lower end of First Avenue. The area was littered with humdrum businesses, from auto repair shops to insurance peddlers, pawnshops to hair salons. There was even an "adult emporium" across the street if we needed a toy or trinket to jump-start our baby-making efforts. It reminded me of Seedier Rapids.

I usually worked the lunch shift. It was nothing like the Harvard Square Pub. The diner lacked even the slightest hint of charm. If the Harvard Square Pub was an elegantly decaying old lady, as Jake used to say, Mel's was a mangy slut. It was held together with spit and duct tape. When it rained, water filtered through the roof and drained into a bucket in the middle of the kitchen floor. Fortunately, it rarely rains in Tucson, and we hid the bucket when the health inspectors came by. Somehow, Mel always seemed to know exactly when they'd visit, before which the entire staff would be obliged to come in early to spiff the place up, discarding the bucket and all other evidence of disrepair.

Mel's was no dream job. I took it because I thought it would be temporary, a paying diversion until the pee stick read positive. But it never did.

I'd been at Mel's for about nine months when things got testy at home. Have you ever heard of a guy getting pissed off because he's getting too much sex? "Not tonight, honey, I'm tired," he'd say, having worked late. I began to wonder if I still turned him on. "Of course you do, Kate," he'd insist, "but you're wearing me out."

The late nights became more frequent. Was it to avoid having sex with me? Or, God forbid, was he having sex with someone else? I broached the subject gingerly. First, I asked him what he'd been working on. I could've cared less, but I thought if I started with that line of inquiry, I could address what was really on my mind. So, I asked him who he was working with.

"Christie Loring," he said. "You remember, you met her at the firm party a few months back."

"You mean the hot young brunette with the pretty smile and big tits? That Christie Loring?"

"Uh . . . yeah, Kate, *that* Christie Loring," he said.

"Hmmm . . ."

He turned his head and gave me his *what-the-fuck* look. "Whaddya mean 'hmmm'?"

"Just hmmm."

Now, I've never, *ever*, been a jealous person and I'd never even imagined Jake with another woman, but suddenly it entered the realm of possibility. Not likelihood, mind you, just possibility. Jake couldn't appreciate how the circumstantial evidence might give a reasonable woman pause. I was, he claimed, no longer a 'reasonable woman.' There was no sex that night either.

Jake got angry when I told him I'd made an appointment for us at a fertility clinic. "Just to make sure there's nothing wrong," I said.

"Jesus, Kate, these things don't happen overnight. Why can't you be patient?"

"I'm not getting any younger, Jake, and neither are you." He slammed a few doors in frustration, but accompanied me to the clinic. The news wasn't bad, per se, but it did suggest that Jake had a case of underperforming sperm. Mobility, motility . . . something like that. Not a major issue, the doctor assured us, just "keep on trucking," he said with a chuckle. I actually found that irritating. He's a fertility doctor and he can't even say the F-word!

Well, I can say it . . . and we did it. Double-time. And the more sex we had, the less satisfying it became. I used to pride myself on my prowess in bed (I was, after all, a porn star, wasn't I?), but it was becoming little more than a means to an end. I felt as if I was dragging him along by the balls, kicking and screaming. I read up on diets, yoga, everything I could think of to help things along. Sure, some of it was a little out of the ordinary, but it was all for a good cause. It was for us, for our future, for our family. And the more I tried, the angrier he got.

The IVF was our last resort. It was difficult and expensive. But it was me who had to deal with all the discomfort, not him. All he had to do was jerk off. And he couldn't even do that sometimes . . . couldn't even get a fucking erection!

CHAPTER THIRTEEN

Jake

I'd like to think that it played no role in her hiring. After all, she was bright, proper, and presentable without taking "it" into account. A native of Austin, Texas, she was poised to graduate with honors from the law school at the University of Texas in May of 2011, just a month prior to the departure of the young associate she'd be hired to replace. She'd hoped to concentrate in the kind of business practice I'd inherited from Nick's father after his retirement. On paper, she was a perfect fit. But there was one minor complication: Christie Loring was a knockout.

"And that's exactly why we shouldn't hire her," Nick argued, as we sat at the conference table after her interviews. "She's bound to be a distraction." Nick had already labeled her "The Babe," a moniker that had nothing to do with her academic qualifications and everything to do with her trim, athletic, five-foot-eight-inch frame, pleasing bust, and killer ass. Not to mention her medium-length dark brown hair, dark eyes, deliciously pouty lips, and dimpled chin. Nick favored making an offer to another candidate—the one he called "The Kid." The Kid, whom I hadn't met, was allegedly a local boy, a 2010 grad from the law school at the University of Arizona, a long-time friend of the family, "a sure bet," Nick insisted.

"Since when is attractiveness an impediment to employment?" I asked.

"Listen, Jake. I just met The Babe," he said, "but I *know* The Kid. I've known him for years. Comes from a good family."

"We're not arranging a marriage, we're hiring an associate."

"You go home every night to a beautiful woman, Jake. Isn't that enough?"

"Irrelevant, Your Honor," I protested. "Besides, whomever we hire will be working primarily with me and, if it may please the Court, I'm partial to Christie—and *not* because she just happens to be, as you allege, a babe."

"It's a damn good thing no one else is listening to this. We'd both get our asses sued."

"By whom, the American Association of Unemployed Babes? Or the Boy Scouts of America?"

"Depends upon whom we pick."

"Let me ask you this, Nick. If your father were sitting at this table, whom would he choose?"

"That's easy," Nick said. "The Babe . . . and for all the wrong reasons. He's a sexist pig."

"What about the "friend of the family" shit? Didn't he know The Kid, too?"

"Nah. I made all that crap up. There is no Kid," Nick said with a big smile. "Just wanted to make sure we were hiring Christie for all the *right* reasons."

"Sometimes, Nick, you can be a royal pain in the ass."

Christie joined Davis, Davis & Singer a month later. She proved a quick study, and I was happy to take her under my wing. Before long, she was indispensable. But working with Christie posed its own set of perils.

Christie had been with us a year when we drove together to Flagstaff to complete a client's acquisition of a manufacturing business. We'd planned to return that evening, but the closing was postponed until the following morning. Rooms were arranged for us at the Drury Inn on the edge of the campus of Northern Arizona University, not far from downtown Flagstaff.

Complications in the transaction necessitated additional drafting and document review. I ordered up room service, and Christie joined me in my room for a working session that lasted well into the evening.

Working closely together for the past year, Christie and I had developed a warm and honest personal relationship. Six years my junior, she was witty, mature, and easy to talk to. Her work habits and work product were first rate, and clients trusted her as much as I did. But, as Nick had predicted, she could be—through no fault of her own—a "distraction."

Our firm consisted of seven lawyers and an equal number of staff. Nick had complained on several occasions about my apparent monopolization of Christie's time, but it was unavoidable, at least in my view. My business practice was expanding rapidly, and Christie had little interest in becoming involved in Nick's practice, mostly trusts and estates. Our other two partners were litigators who'd already invested several years of time and training in the firm's other two associates.

"I'm concerned," Nick said to me early one evening, slipping into my office at the end of the day. He helped himself to the chair opposite my desk.

"About what, Nick?"

"About you and Christie."

"What about me and Christie?"

"She's obviously enamored of you, Jake." He picked up a baseball resting atop a stack of files on the corner of my desk, rotating it absent-mindedly in the palm of his hand. It was a remnant from a past life, darkened from years of handling.

"You spend too much time together as it is, and . . ." He didn't complete the sentence, but I knew where he was heading.

Nick was forever looking out for me and, as the son of the founder of DD&S, the legacy of the firm. We'd talked often about my troubles with Kate. He knew I was unhappy at home. While he admired and respected Christie, he was convinced, along with many others in the firm, that she'd developed a crush on me. He saw her as a looming threat to my marriage and, in a worst-case scenario, to the equilibrium of the firm.

"She adores you, Jake," he said, flicking the baseball back and forth. "And I know you feel the same way about her. I understand . . . it would be hard to feel otherwise . . . she's a terrific lawyer, a wonderful person, and she's—"

"A babe?"

"Right, Jake, a babe."

I wasn't oblivious. If the truth be told, I'd harbored similar fears. But it was those very concerns that had kept me in check. And it was not as if Christie had done anything even remotely inappropriate to encourage me. She was simply being her competent, charming, friendly self. I figured it best to hear Nick out.

"I'm afraid there'll come a time," he said, "when the dam of all that repressed mutual admiration is going to break, wreaking devastation on your marriage and risk to the firm."

I applauded him for his elegant metaphor. "I'm not going to insult your intelligence—or our friendship—by suggesting you're entirely off base," I said, rubbing my palms across my temples. "Nothing you've said is a revelation. I appreciate your concerns, but I think I'm more than capable of dealing with the temptation. I've done so successfully to this point. And Christie's been completely and utterly professional."

"I hope so," he said, squeezing the baseball in his right palm.

"And I hope I haven't offended you by raising this."

"Not at all, buddy . . . or should I say 'Mom'?"

Nick rose from the chair, flipping the ball across the desk into my hands. We both chuckled, a bit awkwardly, and not without some lingering fear that his prophecy might come to pass, that his metaphorical dam would ultimately crack, break, and bring a world of hurt upon us all.

That night in the hotel room with Christie was the biggest test of our mutual resolve. When we'd finished our work, I invited her to join me for a drink at the lobby bar. I owed her that, I thought. It also got us out of the hotel room.

After a round of drinks, I took a calculated risk. I told Christie about my conversation with Nick. I addressed its implications as objectively as I could.

"You're a pleasure to work with," I told her, "and you're smart and talented. But I don't want our close working relationship—or our friendship—to be misinterpreted, either in the office or out. I don't want anyone imagining anything inappropriate between us."

Christie was unfazed by my remarks. "I won't deny my admiration for you as a person, Jake," she said in her soft Texas drawl, her right hand wrapped firmly around her bourbon and water, "but I have no desire to ruin a wonderful working relationship, much less your marriage. I get where Nick's coming from, but there's no need for any concern about me."

The conversation we didn't have would have been more revealing.

"I've wanted you, Jake, since the moment I met you," she'd have said. *"This restraint is driving me crazy!"*

"Wife? What wife?" I'd have replied. *"Let's go and get laid!"*

In the end, only the ground rules were laid.

CHAPTER FOURTEEN

Kate

I grew up Lutheran. I didn't choose it; it was chosen for me by my great grandfather, Timothy Olson, nearly a century earlier. According to family legend, he was orphaned in Sweden at eight, his parents perishing in a fire that he allegedly set. His survival was hailed as a miracle. But with no siblings, and relatives hesitant to embrace a budding juvenile delinquent, he was dumped at the nearest orphanage, which happened to be Catholic.

A rebellious teenager, he pissed off the nuns at every turn. They rewarded him with the whip. He bolted the orphanage at sixteen, found his way into steerage, and came to America.

Great Grandpa Olson worked—and drank—himself halfway across the country. A wrong turn at Cedar Rapids stranded him in Butte Rock. Catching on as a farm hand, he knocked up the farmer's daughter. The shotgun wedding took place in the Lutheran church, which suited him fine, since the other church was Catholic.

Every Sunday morning from that day forward, Great Grandpa Olson and all of his descendants attended the very same Immanuel Lutheran Church in which Jake and I were married. It was programmed into our DNA. Like breathing.

Truth is, I'd never given religion much thought. It was just there, like Friday night football.

Jake, on the other hand, was an anti-religious snob. That, too, had passed down in his family. His parents had no tolerance for blind faith of any kind.

So if I wanted to practice my religion, or *any* religion, I'd be on my own. Lacking passion or commitment, I let it lapse—until the pressure of our failures at baby-making became more than I could bear. By then, I needed support, encouragement, and a reason for optimism. Jake no longer offered me that.

Two churches stood nearby. One was Catholic, the other, The Good News Church, was one of those so-called "non-denominational" churches. Attending the Catholic Church would have been an insult to Great Grandpa Olson. So, on a whim, I arose one Sunday morning and dressed for a visit to The Good News Church.

"Where're you going?" Jake asked, still lying in bed, watching me dress. The sun was just peeking through the bedroom window.

"I'm going to church." My tone was defiant.

"Just like that?" He sat up, staring at me.

"I've been thinking about it for a while."

"You haven't said anything."

"I knew you wouldn't approve."

Jake gave me one of those looks of exasperation that had become increasingly common. "Why?"

"Because I need some hope, some encouragement."

"About what?" he asked, though he knew full well what was bothering me.

"What do you think?"

"The baby thing." That was the demeaning way he'd come to refer to it.

"Right, Sherlock," I said, with a long sigh. "Are you really this dense or just pretending to be?"

"Okay, okay," he said. "What church?"

I told him. He was unimpressed, but refrained from saying anything he'd regret. While he dragged himself out of bed and got dressed, I grabbed a bite and attended church for the first time since our wedding day.

The Good News was a far cry from the Immanuel Lutheran. They talked about the "divine self" and the "inner Godhead," whatever that meant. Referred to God and Jesus, but in untraditional ways. I couldn't tell what, exactly, they believed in, but they didn't force-feed me anything either. A bit loosey-goosey, perhaps, but with an energy that appealed to me.

Pastor Peter Becker presided over the congregation. In his early thirties, he was dynamic and handsome. His features were soft—more delicate than rugged. He conducted the service like a game show host, prodding his parishioners to actively participate. Now and then he'd offer a comment, issue a warning, or spin a moral lesson.

After the service ended and most of the congregation had filed out, the pastor approached me. "I don't believe I've had the pleasure of meeting you," he said. I introduced myself. Told him it was my first visit.

"I take pride in getting to know my parishioners," he said. "Helps me to be of service. Perhaps," he suggested, "I can persuade you to join me for coffee some time during the upcoming week, so we can become better acquainted?"

It seemed like a sincere and generous invitation, so I accepted.

Pastor Becker was already seated at an outdoor table with a couple of coffees when I arrived at the Daily Grind on Fourth Avenue. He greeted me warmly, pulled out a chair, and handed me a cup.

"Thought you might be a cappuccino girl, but if you prefer

something else—"

"No, no, that's perfect."

"Tell me something about yourself," he began. "Are you new to Tucson?"

I told him about growing up in Iowa, about moving to Cambridge, marrying Jake, and relocating to Tucson. Like me, he'd been raised in the Plains—Kansas, in his particular case. He was easy to talk to and listened intently to everything I said.

"Do you have children?" he asked. I shook my head, but the look in my eyes expressed my anguish. "Is that the hollowness in your life," he asked, "that moved you to visit us on Sunday?" His words were gentle and sympathetic. I nodded.

"We've been trying for over two years. We've tried everything," I said, my desperation obvious. "It's destroying me," I admitted, "as well as our marriage."

I began tearing up. I couldn't help it. He reached out and squeezed my hand. "I'm glad you joined us Sunday. You're not alone, Kate." He stared into my eyes with compassion. "There are others in our congregation who suffer the very same pain," he assured me. "I've thought about starting a support group for parishioners going through what you're experiencing. Would that interest you, Kate?"

"Absolutely!" I dabbed the corners of my eyes with a tissue and returned to my coffee.

"I'll make a few calls, and I'll let you know more after next week's service. You'll be there?"

"I wouldn't miss it." I finished my cappuccino and rose to leave. "Thank you, Pastor Becker," I said. "It's been a comfort just talking with you."

"My pleasure, Kate." He smiled warmly. "And please call me Peter." He grasped my hand again as we rose from the table. "God bless you."

CHAPTER FIFTEEN

Jake

Religion. That's what nearly put the kibosh on our marriage. Kate had the curious notion that it could solve all our problems. Nothing else had.

This was hardly welcome news to me. I'd always harbored an aversion to organized religion, an aversion as powerful as Kate's compulsion to reproduce. The product of an agnostic household, the only time I or any other member of our family ventured within a church or synagogue was for a wedding or funeral. Of course, one might argue that The Good News Church was more accurately categorized as *disorganized* religion. It was one of those congregations led by a pastor on steroids, or maybe ecstasy, where everyone shouts out whatever enters their minds, like a convention of Tourette's patients. And the Good News Church had a decidedly bad news pastor, the Pastor Peter Becker, whom I mockingly referred to as Pastor Bastard, much to Kate's annoyance. To mollify her, I attended one Sunday service. That's how I know what a crock it was.

"I'm not going back to that circus," I told her the moment we exited the front door of the saucer-shaped church building.

"Fine, asshole. I'll go alone." And she did.

One day early in her religious phase, while she was still talking to me, Kate announced that she was joining a church support group for childless couples. She asked me to accompany her.

"What, so Pastor Bastard can rub our noses in it?"

"He'll pray for us, Jake."

"He'll prey *on* us, Kate."

I should have swallowed my pride and joined her, but I didn't.

It wasn't long after she'd begun attending the sessions that her behavior changed. Kate stopped making sexual demands. There were no more turkey-baster attacks, no more invective demeaning my manhood. She even displayed occasional flashes of the girl I married.

"It's the church group," she told me. "Pastor Becker makes me feel like I'm worth something again."

"Whoever suggested you weren't?"

"You won't even fuck me anymore!"

"We haven't made love like normal people in ages," I reminded her.

"So, I'm not normal?" And so on. She was happier, but not necessarily with me.

Kate attended Pastor Bastard's support group meetings with increasing frequency, or so it appeared. And since she'd recently quit her waitressing job—without explanation—I'd no way of knowing how much time she was spending at church. But I was becoming curious.

Despite the understanding I'd forged with Christie in Flagstaff—or maybe because of it—I found myself sharing with her the trials and tribulations of my personal life. Our relationship had become almost sibling-like; she was a constructive and sympathetic listener. I'd told her about Kate's sessions at the Good News Church and my unease with the frequency of her visits.

"I just don't trust that guy," I told her as we consumed a Chinese take-out dinner during a late-night work session at the office. "Why does her group meet so damn often?"

"Why be suspicious of a group meeting?" she asked.

"I don't know, Christie. She talks about this guy way too much. Makes me uncomfortable."

"Don't you trust Kate?"

I should have been able to answer that question easily, but for some reason, I hesitated. What cause did I have to distrust her? She'd been forthright about her visits to the church—even urged me to join her. Was it the unexplained drop-off in her urgency for sex? Or was I simply flummoxed by her sudden and resolute embrace of religion?

"Look," Christie said, "maybe I can help you sort this out." She put down her chopsticks. "What if I do some undercover work at the church? I can borrow a ring and sit down with your Pastor Bastard. I'll find out just what he offers and how often."

"I can't ask you to do something like that."

"Really, Jake, it's no big deal. Anyway, I'm curious to meet this Pastor Bastard you're always talking about."

"You won't call him that, will you?"

"Not unless he deserves it."

I felt uneasy about both what I'd revealed to Christie and what, in a moment of weakness and frustration, I'd agreed to allow her to do. I worried that she'd run into Kate, or that Pastor Bastard would sniff out the ruse and report it to Kate. It was a really stupid idea and I regretted it almost as much then as I do now. But I didn't abort it, even though I could have.

Christie took off early that Friday afternoon. Donning a wedding ring she'd borrowed from a friend, she met with Pastor Bastard. She posed as a housewife unable to conceive. Like the good associate that she was, she wrote me a memo:

To: JS
From: CL
Date: February 15, 2013
Re: The "Parents Awaiting Pregnancy" Support Group

I met late this afternoon with Pastor Peter Becker of the Good News Church. Posing as a married woman frustrated in her attempts to become pregnant, I inquired about the PAP Support Group. Pastor Becker indicated that, as of a couple of months ago, the group no longer meets formally, but that he personally counsels support group members on a one-to-one basis as often as circumstances require.

What she didn't put in the memo she told me when she delivered it on Monday morning.

"Pastor Bastard spent more time eyeing my bust than my face," Christie said. "I wouldn't trust him with anyone's wife."

That night, I confronted Kate about the support group meetings. She was unusually defensive. She admitted that her meetings were no longer of the group variety.

"So how often do you meet with Pastor Bastard?" My tone was unduly accusatory.

"I told you to stop calling him that!"

"Okay, Pastor Becker."

"It varies. Two, maybe three times a week." I rolled my eyes while she snarled.

"What do you do at these meetings?"

"Read scripture, pray, talk about God's healing."

"Pray for what?"

"For the Red Sox to win the pennant," she barked. "What do you *think* we pray for? What've we been trying desperately to do for the last two years?"

"When do you meet with him next?"

"Wednesday at four. Wanna come along? It would do us both some good."

I took that as a bluff. "No thanks, Kate. You go on alone. If it's helping you cope, fine. You certainly seem a good deal happier lately." She smiled weakly while I made plans for a clandestine visit to the Good News Church.

I borrowed Christie's car on Wednesday and drove to the church. I couldn't believe what I was doing. I was acting like a jealous asshole, but I couldn't help myself. I was there early, but Kate's car was already in the parking lot. There was one other vehicle in the lot. I slinked into the building like a gumshoe in a Bogart movie. If anything went awry, I could simply say that I'd reconsidered and had come to participate in the four o'clock session.

I found the Pastor's office and knocked on the door. No answer. I pressed on.

I located the stairs to the lower level. Ahead, a noise. Something falling to the floor—a book, maybe a sheath of papers. I traced the sound down a hallway to a meeting room. The door was shut. Behind it, gasps and moans. Was I imagining this? I was loath to credit the unspeakable conclusion that was brewing in my mind.

Gently, I turned the doorknob. The door was locked. I pondered my options. I could smash the door in. Pro: if Pastor Bastard was screwing my wife behind this door, I'd catch them red-handed. Con: if not, I'd risk arrest for breaking and entering and have the challenge of my life explaining my actions to police, pastor, and Kate. I could knock, but that would give them a chance to collect themselves or, more likely, take refuge behind the locked door.

Yogi Berra purportedly said: "when you come to a fork in the road, take it." I'd arrived at that fork. It was one of those moments I could regret for the rest of my life, like the day I blew out my elbow, the day I surrendered my index finger to a Mafia-wannabe, or the day I willfully ignored the counsel of my father and married Kate. A voice in my head told me, in no uncertain terms, to walk away. But what was I walking away from? Confrontation? Knowledge? Marriage? My marriage was in shambles. What did I have to lose?

I knocked. I waited five emotionally charged seconds. Hearing frantic whispering and scurrying, I reverted to the first of my options, smashing the door completely off its hinges. The crash was deafening.

My jaw slackened. There they stood, their eyes frozen in panic as I confronted them, Pastor Bastard zipping his pants and Kate desperately fumbling with her bra straps.

"It's not what you think!" Kate shrieked, a look of abject terror etched on her face.

"Of course it is!" I said, turning away in disgust, retracing my steps down the hallway and up the stairs, out the door, and into the parking lot.

CHAPTER SIXTEEN

Kate

"I did it for you!" I cried when he walked in the door that evening. It was the worst day of my life. I'd been bawling non-stop, curled in a corner of the living room, searching for a way to express what I knew to be true. I wasn't sure if Jake would come home. I didn't know what I'd do if he did . . . or what to do if he didn't.

"*What* did you say?" Four words dripping with accusation and anger.

"Pastor Becker thought that if his sperm could do the job yours couldn't, we'd still have our baby, and you wouldn't need to know how it took place," I babbled, "and you'd have no reason to doubt it was yours!" I was a sniveling wreck. I'd chosen the wrong words, words that belittled Jake. I was making a bad situation worse, but I couldn't shut up. Jake collapsed onto the living room couch like a sack of potatoes. "At first I said no," I went on, barely pausing to breathe, "but it made sense, Jake. I thought if I got pregnant, it would save our marriage!"

"What a crock of shit!" he roared. "This marriage is a fucking joke!" I guess I deserved that.

"I'm sorry, Jake. I'm *so* very sorry. But you have to believe me! There's nothing between the Pastor and me. I swear!"

Jake was livid. "We could have gone the donor route, Kate.

It would have been simple, straightforward." Tears formed in his eyes as he lashed out at me. I couldn't blame him. He was right—we could have done it another way.

"All I wanted was to make a baby for you . . . for both of us," I explained, for the umpteenth time, through a veil of tears. "To go back to the way we were . . . before all this."

It was an unusual plan, to be sure. Peter had broached the subject several weeks earlier. Our previous session had yielded more than my usual quota of tears.

"You were in so much pain the last time we met," Peter said, sitting across from me in his office. "After you left, I prayed for guidance. And that night, I had a vivid, but troubling, dream." He hesitated, as if debating whether to continue.

"A dream about me?"

"Yes," he said. "It offered a solution. At first, I found it disturbing, but then I recognized its logic." He rubbed his chin, pausing again.

"Come on, Peter, get to the point!"

"I'll tell you in a moment, Kate. But first I want you to understand that this was a dream . . . a divine message, I believe . . . but not one I could have devised on my own. It is, to say the least, highly unorthodox."

Okay, he really had me going now. "Are you going to tell me or not?"

"God implored me to impregnate you with my seed."

"What?"

"A simple, pragmatic solution. No emotional entanglement. You conceive a child. Your husband believes that it's his—and, for all intents and purposes, it is. And who's to say that it *isn't* his seed that impregnates you, anyway?"

I know how this sounds. I was shocked when he made the suggestion. It seemed inconceivable—no pun intended. But I trusted the pastor implicitly. So, as bizarre and unexpected as this proposal was, I couldn't dismiss it. I told him I'd think it over. And I did.

Jake and I had considered using the sperm of a donor. I knew he was willing, but his heart wasn't in it. With Peter's approach, Jake would assume that the child was his. And, as Peter noted, who's to say it's *not* Jake's sperm that does the trick? Yes, I'd be deceiving Jake, but for all the right reasons. We'd have our child, and Jake and I could resume living the lives we'd envisioned. I'd had sex with many men before Jake, often without emotional commitment. Then, it was recreation; now, a means to an end. It didn't *mean* anything, aside from what it might achieve. But none of that planning figured on Jake pounding a door down to catch us in action.

Jake lifted himself wearily from the couch. He walked right past me, down the hall, and into the bedroom. I heard him yank his suitcase from his closet, then open and shut the drawers of his bureau. I followed him into the bedroom. "Don't leave, Jake," I pleaded. "Please!"

Jake zipped up the suitcase, grabbed a few suits. He passed me without so much as a glance; didn't utter a single word. And then he was gone.

CHAPTER SEVENTEEN

Jake

I drove to a hotel on Grant. My mind was racing. What's a guy supposed to do when he catches his wife fucking her pastor? I'd condensed my new reality into a fractured nursery rhyme, with apologies to Mother Goose: *Pastor Peter Becker put his pecker in Kate's pussy!* The words rattled through my brain like a rat ensnared in a maze.

I wanted to return to the Good News Church and smash the living daylights out of Pastor Bastard. I realized, of course, it would accomplish little more than to assuage my badly bruised ego. It wouldn't take much to kill the bastard, but I didn't need to make my putrid life even worse by spending it behind bars. And if I did make a scene, word of Kate's indiscretion—a wholly inadequate word for what she'd done—would become public, embarrassing us both even further. There was only one person with whom I could discuss this, the person who understood why I made the pilgrimage to the Good News Church in the first place.

From my hotel room, I called Christie's cell. It rang four times before she picked up.

"It's Jake," I said. "I need to talk. Can you meet me for a drink?" Though surprised by the invitation, she agreed at once, not even pausing to request an explanation. She knew, of course, that I'd gone to the church that afternoon. "The 21 Club . . . on Fourth. Meet you there in half an hour."

I was sitting at the bar nursing my second scotch when Christie arrived. I'd imagined her dressed in a tee shirt and shorts when I'd called. If so, she'd upgraded her wardrobe significantly for this dubious encounter. She wore her hair down, probably reapplied some lipstick, and donned a satiny white blouse over a chic pair of jeans. Heads turned as she approached my barstool.

"What's up, Jake?" she asked breezily, camouflaging her curiosity.

"Let's move this to a table." I asked her what she wanted to drink and placed the order with the barman.

"Sorry for dragging you out like this," I said, "but I had to talk to someone."

"Kate?" she surmised. "And the Pastor?"

"Uh . . ." I blurted out the indelicate words of my tacky tongue twister: "*Pastor Peter Becker put his pecker in Kate's pussy!*" I delivered the pronouncement without the hint of a smile.

"Whaaat?" She didn't know whether to laugh, commiserate with me, or ask me to repeat what she thought she'd heard. Instead, she looked at me stoically, waiting for confirmation that I'd actually meant what I'd said.

"Sorry," I said, reinforcing myself with a gulp of scotch, "I shouldn't be so flippant. It's been a difficult day."

"You mean to tell me—"

"Yes. Bad news at the Good News," I said, biting my upper lip. "I caught them *in flagrante delicto.*" She gasped.

I began to relate my story. When I reached the point where I'd trashed the door, she leaned forward and thrust out her palms. "Come on, Jake. Tell me you're joking . . . about *all* of this."

"I wish I was." She sighed, shaking her head in disbelief. I signaled the bartender for refills and continued my saga. Christie listened intently, barely touching her second drink.

"Have you been home? Have you talked to Kate?"

I recounted the details of my brief conversation with Kate, as well as her convoluted justification for the entire fiasco. Christie was speechless.

"I don't know what to say, Jake." She clutched my hand from across the table. Her touch was warm and comforting. "Are you okay?"

"Not yet," I admitted, my eyes melting into her gaze. I saw compassion in her deep brown eyes, for which I was sorely in need.

"Are you going home tonight?" It was an innocent question pregnant with perils and possibilities. Would she invite me to spend the night at her place? If she did, would I accept?

"I've checked into a hotel." I felt a tidal wave of relief having said it.

For the next two hours, we talked, drank, even joked about Pastor Peter Becker's errant pecker. She raised my spirits and eased my anguish. For that, I was deeply grateful.

CHAPTER EIGHTEEN

Kate

I was shaking when I checked the pee stick. There had been nothing more I'd wanted for the last two years than to be pregnant, but not now. Not with all that had just taken place. A pregnancy now would be devastating.

You can't imagine my relief when I realized I'd dodged that bullet. But the wounds that preceded it might well have been fatal. I called Jake's cell phone all weekend. I left messages. *Call me, Jake, please. Let me know you're okay. Tell me where you are.* Sometimes all I could do was cry.

For two full days, Jake maintained radio silence. On Monday morning, I called his office. My call went directly to voicemail. Had he even come in? I tried Nick. At least he picked up. I had no idea whether Nick knew what had taken place over the last several days.

"Nick, have you seen Jake?" I tried to avoid sounding distraught. "I haven't been able to reach him all morning."

"Saw him earlier," he said, "with Christie. Is everything okay?" He seemed unaware of our blow-up. He promised Jake would return my call. He didn't.

Two hours later, I drove to Jake's office. I figured he'd see me, if only to avoid a scene. I was right.

Jake motioned me into his office and shut the door. His face was blank as snow.

"Where are you staying?"

"The Marriott on Grant."

"Do you need anything?"

"No, Kate, I'm fine." We sat there for a good thirty seconds, staring at each other, neither saying a word.

I broke the stalemate. "Can we talk about this?"

"Don't think I'm ready," he said.

I didn't press. Didn't feel I had the right. "I love you, Jake. I was worried." I reached for his hand; he recoiled from my touch. My heart sank even further. "I'm glad you're okay," I said, rising to leave. He made no effort to stop me. I flashed a fake smile to Jake's secretary as I headed down the corridor. I couldn't help but notice Christie Loring, standing by her secretary's desk. She was staring at me. I could tell that she knew.

The next day, Jake sent me a text. "Meet me tonight. Tavolino @ 6."

I found him seated at a quiet table in the back of the restaurant. Bow-tied waiters scurried among tables covered with white tablecloths. Jake had finished one scotch; another was on its way. A glass of Chardonnay had been set at my place. He'd already ordered us dinner.

I didn't know what to say, or why he'd arranged this meeting. He looked more weary than angry. My knees trembled; tears welled in my eyes. I refused to cry.

"Tell me honestly, Kate," he said, speaking in hushed tones, "do you love him?"

"God, Jake, no . . . *absolutely not*!"

His next question was more difficult. "How many times?"

I felt compelled to answer. "Six, maybe seven." He grimaced.

"Are you pregnant?"

"No. I've checked. No." A sigh of relief.

"Whose idea was it," he asked pointedly, "his or yours?"

"His."

The waiter delivered that second scotch. Jake reached for the glass immediately, fortifying himself with a healthy swig. He gave me a scolding look. "How could you think it was even *remotely* acceptable?"

I'd answered this question before. He'd found my explanation wanting. "I was desperate," I told him again. "Our failures at baby-making were ruining our marriage. I trusted him. He offered a solution." I paused for more wine. "If I got pregnant, you'd never doubt it was yours. And we'd be good again, like we were in the beginning." The more I explained it, the more foolish it sounded.

Jake clutched his drink in both hands, staring at the melting ice. "How could you live with yourself," he asked, his eyes betraying his anguish, "deceiving me like that?"

I had no clue how to respond to that question. I shook my head slowly, my eyes cast downward, saying nothing. I hadn't the nerve to meet his gaze. He didn't know the half of it—didn't know the real reason I'd left Iowa. I'd been deceiving him from the day we met. Part of me wanted to tell him everything, but I couldn't. It would be the death of our marriage—if it wasn't already over.

He released his grip on his scotch, placing his hand on mine. "Do you love me, Kate?"

"Absolutely!"

He smiled weakly. But the interrogation wasn't over. He glared at me before unleashing one last question. "Do you believe I'm having an affair with Christie?"

I didn't expect that one. He could feel my hesitation. "It

crossed my mind," I admitted sheepishly. Jake released my hand, biting his lip. "I couldn't have blamed you," I quickly explained, "the way our marriage was collapsing. But deep down," I added, "I don't think I really believed it." I had no idea what was going to come next.

It was the lasagna.

CHAPTER NINETEEN

Jake

The day after our dinner at Tavolino's, I moved back home. Not because all was forgiven, and not because it didn't hurt anymore. The longer I avoided Kate, the harder it would be to repair what had broken. She'd been gullible, foolish, and reckless, but her remorse seemed genuine. I was willing to try, at least, to forgive her, but on my own terms and timetable. Both of us longed for a semblance of normalcy.

But the life we'd resumed wasn't normal. Our conversations were mired in banalities. "Going to the grocery store, Jake. Anything you want?" she'd ask. "It's trash day," I'd announce. "Anything else to throw out?" We flitted about as if treading on eggshells. Neither of us had the courage or energy to address the elephant roaming the house like a rampaging mastodon. She'd look at me with the eyes of a doe, a look that telegraphed both fear and vulnerability. I made it no easier for her, wearing my cuckold mask and moping about like a sullen teenager.

The greatest awkwardness came at bedtime. At first, neither of us made a move, as if enforcing a conjugal no-fly zone in compliance with an unwritten treaty. We'd each say 'goodnight,' maybe even a perfunctory 'love you,' then tumble in opposite directions, retreating behind our respective battle lines.

Two weeks into our standoff, the ice finally broke. As I sat in bed reading, Kate emerged from the bathroom in a sexy morsel of lacy black lingerie, a sure aphrodisiac in better times. Silently, she slipped beneath the covers, reaching over timidly to touch me. Part of me recoiled, the part that Kate had betrayed. Part of me didn't, the part that she'd often referred to giddily as my misplaced digit. The next move was up to me.

I'd almost forgotten how alluring Kate could be. For so long, our lovemaking had been compromised, the pure joy and emotion of the act becoming lost in her obsession with reproduction. Now, her eyes implored me as urgently as her body enticed me. We were tentative, like teenagers exploring each other's bodies for the very first time. And, like teenage sex, it was awkward, until the once familiar rhythms regained their traction. As if by tacit agreement, neither of us spoke, our lovemaking more eloquent than words.

When we'd finished, Kate clutched me tightly, like a frightened child gripping her teddy bear. And by morning, that elusive normalcy had returned, snapped into place like a dislocated digit.

It was just a week later, on an early March afternoon, when Nick, as he was wont to do, sauntered into my office to shoot the breeze.

"Take a look at this, Ace," he said, depositing the sports section of the *Daily Star* on my desk, folded open to the third page. He'd drawn a big red circle around a small article announcing tryouts for the Tucson Scorpions, the local franchise in the Tex-Ar-Mex League, a newly-organized, independent, semi-pro baseball league composed of teams from Arizona, New Mexico and western Texas.

"You're kidding, right?"

"Not at all, Jake. You should try out."

"Jesus, Nick! I haven't thrown seriously for over a decade. I'm thirty-three years old! The guys that go out for these teams are in their late teens, early twenties. Plus, I already have a job, or hadn't you noticed?"

"Your arm's had a long vacation," Nick observed. "No wear and tear—that's good. And you could limit yourself to home games, all of which are played at night." He'd done his homework.

"What makes you think I can even control a pitch with this fucked-up hand?"

"What makes you think you can't?"

Nick lectured me on the exploits of Mordecai "Three-Finger" Brown, a baseball Hall-of-Famer who won 239 games pitching mostly for the Chicago Cubs at the dawn of the twentieth century. "Mangled his hand in a farm accident as a kid. Developed one of the most devastating curveballs in baseball history. And he had one less digit than you!"

"Gimme a break," I said, scoffing at the absurdity of what Nick was suggesting.

"That's exactly what I'm trying to do."

CHAPTER TWENTY

Jake

The night we'd made love again was transformative. It was the first time—in a long time—that we were back to square one, the way we'd felt about each other in Cambridge, before the "baby thing" hijacked our life.

We came to an understanding on that subject the next morning. Kate got up early, dressed, and decamped to the kitchen. She whipped up a country breakfast like she had the morning after our first night together. The fragrance of freshly baked blueberry muffins roused me from bed and into the kitchen. I crept up behind her, grazing her neck with a kiss.

"Last night was nice," I whispered into her ear, as she flipped the sizzling bacon in the skillet.

She turned to me and smiled. "Yeah," she purred, "and that's the way it'll be from now on, right, lover?" I nodded my endorsement.

Completing her elaborate preparations, Kate filled my dish with farmhouse delicacies, and sat down with a plate of her own. I interrupted our bliss to address a still touchy subject.

"Kate, we need to come to an agreement." She looked at me nervously, fidgeting with her fork. "I'd like to propose that for the next six months, we make love like we did last night, without any thought about baby-making. And, if you're not pregnant by then, we go the donor route."

Kate flashed a big grin. "You wanna make love for six months? Every night?" She laughed. "Sure, big guy, I can live with that."

It was good to have her back.

While clearing the breakfast dishes, I casually mentioned Nick's campaign to persuade me to return to baseball. I thought she'd be amused.

"You should do it!" Kate said. "Absolutely!"

"Not you, too!"

"What've you got to lose? You miss it," she said. "I *know* you do. You're in great shape, honey, so why not?"

"But—"

"But what? Tryout's not for a few weeks. Go out and throw. See how you feel. You might be pleasantly surprised!"

Kate's enthusiasm was infectious. Of course I missed baseball. I hadn't quit on my own terms. But I'd never given a moment's thought to pitching with a four-fingered hand. And I'd never heard of Mordecai "Three-Finger" Brown.

I stopped in Nick's office the next morning with a proposition.

"Still think you can handle what's left of my fastball?" I asked.

Nick might have been a scrawny little shit, but he was tough. During our Stanford days, he'd often don the catcher's gear to loosen me up, or help me work through some mechanical flaw he'd diagnosed.

"Fuck, yeah!" he crowed.

Nick and I met early that Saturday morning on a nearby high school diamond. It felt good to unearth my old glove again—the same one I'd used through college and my abbreviated professional career; the one I'd employed to conceal the engagement ring I gave Kate on her twenty-first birthday. I felt that same sense of nervous anticipation I recalled from my earliest days at Stanford.

But my excitement was tempered with doubt. I'd quit the game cold turkey. The emotional sting of what I'd lost had kept me away from the game I loved. Was I on the verge of revelation or humiliation? It wouldn't take long to find out.

The field we'd chosen was spartan but serviceable. I strolled to the mound like I had a thousand times before, clutching the ball in my left hand, now one digit short of a quintet. Weeds encroached the perimeter of the mound like algae invading a pond. Gullies carved by legions of hurlers surrounded the pockmarked pitching rubber. It was no Fenway Park, but it felt like home.

Nick stationed himself behind the plate, in front of the chain-link backstop. He wore an old catcher's mitt, mask, and chest protector he'd salvaged from the trash heap after our senior year at Stanford.

"Let's see what you've got, Ace!" Nick cried out, as animated as a teenager.

I fingered the ball tentatively in what remained of my left hand. The "feel" was different than I'd remembered: the grip I'd used in my playing days was no longer feasible. I lobbed a few pitches uncertainly, searching for a comfortable grip. As the feeling of awkwardness dissipated, my velocity increased.

"That stung!" Nick's protest was music to my ears. There was more left in that left arm than I'd realized. Using my thumb, middle, and ring fingers, I could still throw a respectable fastball, though it had a tendency to swerve to the left.

"Adjust your arm angle," Nick suggested. "Come a little

more over the top." His advice, as usual, was spot-on. To enhance the lateral movement, I'd drop the angle down a slot; to straighten it, I'd throw more over the top.

Nick urged me to revisit my breaking ball. It took some doing, but I discovered that wedging the ball against the stub of my index finger, and gripping it with my thumb and middle finger, imparted a dramatic downward break to what, in my earlier pitching days, had been an unremarkable curveball.

Before long, a group of youngsters congregated behind the backstop. Arriving early for a practice of their own, they were intrigued by the old guy throwing heat with a mangled left hand.

"Who *is* this dude?" one of them called to Nick.

"Jake Singer," Nick replied. "Remember that name."

CHAPTER TWENTY-ONE

Kate

In my worst nightmares, I never imagined I'd see Billy Garabedian again. I thought I'd closed that ugly chapter of my life, tossed it out with the trash when I hopped that Greyhound to Boston almost four years earlier. It was early April of 2013, just weeks after our marital reconciliation.

It began like any other day in the desert, sunny and hot, until a nasty bank of clouds rumbled in. The sky exploded, releasing its moisture in torrents. Tucson downpours can be menacing. But not as menacing as what the cat dragged in through the pouring rain.

A car door slammed and the doorbell rang. I opened the door and gasped.

"Hello, Kate," Billy sneered, standing, unprotected, in the drenching rain. It felt as if he'd thrust a knife into my gut. I shuddered, torn between anger and fear. I tried to shut the door in his face, but he resisted, forcing his way in.

I ordered him to leave. He didn't budge, laughing fiendishly while rainwater puddled at his feet. "You've got balls showing up here, you prick!" I screamed.

"That's no way to treat an old lover," Billy said, shaking the rain off his head like a mangy cat. "Either grab me a towel or I'll strip naked right here." I snatched a dirty dishtowel from the kitchen counter and threw it in his face.

"What are you doing here?" I stammered. "How the hell did you find me?"

"It wasn't hard to find you, Kate," he said, patting the rain off his slimy, slicked-back hair. He still wore that stupid 'man bun.' "Traced you back to your mommy and daddy in Butte Rock." My stomach turned somersaults when he mentioned my parents. "Said I was an old friend. They were more than happy to provide your address."

I almost gagged. "You didn't—"

"Tell 'em their sweet little daughter's a porn queen?" Diabolic laughter. "No, Kate. I didn't do that . . . at least not yet."

"Get out!" I was panicking now. "My husband'll be home any minute!" I lied.

"Now, now, Kate. No reason to get all hot and bothered. I'm here with a simple business proposition."

"GET THE FUCK OUT!" I pushed him toward the door. He grabbed my arms and flung me aside. The bastard then strutted right past me into the kitchen, helping himself to a seat at the counter.

"Now, hear me out," Billy said, stiffening. "I've decided to transform a momentary financial shortfall into an irresistible investment opportunity . . . one I thoughtfully designed especially for you." He leaned back on the chair, a self-satisfied smirk plastered across his stubbly face. "I just need a little seed money . . . for the next of my famous love stories. Ten grand'll do the trick, darlin'." He raised his eyebrows and lowered his voice. "Unless, of course, you'd like to star in it instead."

"You fucking bastard! You really think you can show up here and blackmail me?"

"You've got it completely wrong, Kate. Like I said, it's an investment opportunity. Nothing more."

"And if I decline your 'investment opportunity'?"

"No biggie. I'll find another investor. Your husband, perhaps? I'll just email your Oscar-worthy performance to him as an indication of the quality of my work—as well as yours." He sniggered. "I'm sure he'll find it intriguing, don't you think?"

Billy had played me like a fiddle. He'd already deduced that my parents knew nothing of that wretched movie, and now, from my horror at the prospect of his revealing it to Jake, he knew that Jake was clueless, too. He had all the leverage he needed. If I didn't submit, Jake would find out, and everything we'd rebuilt in the last few weeks would shatter into jagged little pieces.

"You are such a fucking low-life! GET OUT!"

"Okay, okay." He stood up. "I can see you're not in a particularly sociable mood today," he said, mocking me. "Your Dad gave me your phone number, so I'll catch you again in . . . shall we say . . . twenty-four hours? You can give me your answer then, okay sweetcheeks?"

Billy swaggered back toward the entryway. "I look forward to our next conversation," he snickered, looking back over his shoulder as he opened the door. Enraged, I rushed at him, shoving him over the threshold and into the rain. I slammed the door so hard the house shook. I ran to the bedroom, threw myself across the bed, and wailed. I felt as helpless as I'd been when Jake caught me with that goddamned Pastor.

What was I supposed to do? If I paid what Billy demanded, he'd leave me alone, but for how long? If I didn't, Jake would surely find out. It'd be the last straw—just when things were right again between us. If I went to the police, I'd have no chance of hiding it from Jake.

I know now what I should have done. I should have leveled with Jake, taken my chances. After all, it happened before we met—and it wasn't my fault, though I should have known better. But I knew how it would look: the embarrassment would be devastating to both of us.

Where could I find ten grand without Jake's knowledge? My mind raced. I could empty my personal checking account, the one I'd set up in Cambridge when I moved there from Iowa—my savings from the Harvard Square Pub. Jake wouldn't notice that. I ran to the den, shuffling through the drawers until I found the checkbook. Hadn't touched it since our marriage. The balance was $5,204.13, barely half of what I needed. Shit! Back to the bedroom. I opened my jewelry box. I could pawn some stuff, right? Things I'd owned before our marriage, things that Jake wouldn't miss. That narrowed it down—a lot. He'd given me most of it—the good stuff, that is. And the rest was probably worthless dreck.

I collected a handful of jewelry, threw it into a little jewelry sack, and hopped into the car. I splashed through the dangerously flooded streets until I reached the pawnshop in the seedy strip mall across from Mel's Diner.

I wiped my tears as I walked in. The aisles overflowed with bric-a-brac. Shelves were layered with electronic equipment. There were enough guitars, horns, drums, woodwinds, and stringed instruments to outfit a high school band.

I made my way to the front counter and placed the jewelry sack on the glass countertop. I wondered at the desperate circumstances that had driven other women to pawn the rings, bracelets, and necklaces that crowded the display case before me.

A fat, balding man rose from the cluttered desk behind the counter. "What've we got here?" A massive birthmark stained his left cheek.

I emptied the sack. I asked what he'd give me for the jewelry I'd poured on the counter. He reached for a loupe, wedging it tightly into his right eye. He pawed through the jewelry like a cat, selecting two or three pieces for closer inspection. "Hmmm," he muttered, grimacing. He put down the loupe and let out a deep, unenthusiastic sigh. "Five bills for the lot."

"Five thousand?"

"No, honey," he laughed. "Five hundred."

I'll admit it: I lost it for a few seconds, sniveling like a baby. The guy was sympathetic, but not enough to raise his offer. I reached into my purse for something to sop up my tears.

"That ring you're wearing," he said, pointing to the engagement ring on my left hand, "can I take a look?" I loved that ring from the moment it tumbled out of Jake's ratty old baseball mitt on my twenty-first birthday. I knew he'd paid dearly for it, though he'd never revealed how much. Reluctantly, I removed the ring and placed it on the countertop. He replaced the loupe in his eye and gazed at the ring. "For *this* I can give you five grand."

I couldn't do that. It was my *engagement ring*, for God's sakes! It was the only ring I ever wore—Jake would surely notice its absence. "I can't do that," I said. And for five hundred, it wasn't worth pawning the rest of it. I thanked the man, reclaimed the ring and my jewelry, and left the shop.

I sat in the car for at least ten minutes fretting, tearfully considering my options. I saw no other way to close the gap. Where else could I go for that kind of money? Then it dawned on me: the ring was insured. I could tell Jake I lost it. He'd be upset, but not nearly as upset as he'd be watching me screw Billy Garabedian for twenty-seven minutes. And if he filed an insurance claim, we could replace the ring.

I opened the car door and reentered the pawnshop. I slipped the ring off my finger and handed it to the fat man. I left with fifty crisp hundred-dollar bills in my purse and a gaping hole in my heart.

CHAPTER TWENTY-TWO

Jake

I called Kate that afternoon to tell her I'd be late for dinner. Nick and I were off to the schoolyard for another workout. I sensed something troubling in her voice—an uncharacteristic breathlessness.

"You okay, Kate?"

"Fine," she said curtly. "See you later."

The throwing session was heartening. I could feel the arm gaining strength. The physical and emotional pleasure of throwing a baseball again—after all these years—triggered long-buried memories of my longing for The Show. The tryout was four days away. It was hardly The Show, but the itch was back.

When I returned home later that evening, Kate was curled up on the couch, her eyes wet and red.

"What is it?" I asked with alarm. "What's wrong?"

"I lost it!" she cried.

"Lost what?"

She raised her left hand, wiggling her bare ring finger. "My engagement ring! *I lost my engagement ring!* God, Jake, I'm *so* sorry!"

I clutched her hand and huddled beside her. She was shaking. I tried to calm her, but to no avail. She was inconsolable. I urged her to mentally reconstruct her day. Where had she been? It seemed, at least according to her testimony that night, that she'd been to just about every retail establishment in the City of Tucson. I suggested she place calls to the shops she'd visited, in case some Good Samaritan had made a fortunate discovery and turned it in. It was too late to begin now, she said, but she'd do so in the morning after I left for work.

"It's insured," I reminded her. "If it doesn't turn up in a few days, we'll put in a claim." She nodded, almost imperceptibly. Kate had never been overly sentimental, so the intensity of her despair both surprised and concerned me.

While Kate struggled to conquer the trauma of the lost ring, Nick and I continued our preparations for the tryout.

I awoke Saturday with butterflies in my stomach. It'd been over a decade since I'd last had that feeling—that last outing in Trenton before the Blues Brothers cut short my index finger and pitching career. Nick was even more excited than I. He picked me up at seven o'clock and peppered me with unsolicited advice all the way to the ballpark.

Tucson Electric Park was abuzz with activity. Just fourteen years old, it was the centerpiece of a state-of-the art spring training complex rudely abandoned by the Chicago White Sox and Arizona Diamondbacks for more lucrative opportunities in Phoenix. Desperate for the tenancy promised by the fledgling Tucson Scorpions, the city fathers had pulled out the stops, unleashing a horde of workers to manicure the field and scrub down the stadium.

My confidence faltered as I peered at the long queue of ballplayers lined up at the registration table. "Not so sure about this, Nick," I muttered.

"Competition is good," Nick assured me. "It'll bring out the best in you." He swatted me in the rump to bolster my fortitude.

"I'm almost old enough to be their father," I said. It was only a slight exaggeration.

"Then you'll be able to teach them a thing or two, Ace."

When we reached the front of the line, I filled out a form—checking off, among other items, the box for "Left-handed pitcher"—and handed it to a gaunt, middle-aged man propped like a garden gnome on a lawn chair behind a card table. He reviewed the form, glancing at the hand that had passed it to him. "Is this a joke?"

"We'll find out soon enough," I replied. He shook his head, gave me a number to pin to my baseball jersey, and directed me to Practice Field A, where a rapidly expanding group of would-be hurlers had gathered beside a row of pitching mounds. A half-dozen men in catching gear idled nearby awaiting instructions. Two older men clutching radar guns stood behind them.

Barney O'Toole was the Scorpions' pitching coach. Ostensibly in his late forties, his tall, lanky frame hinted at a promising professional career cut short, as most inevitably are, by injury, bad luck, or lack of opportunity. Now coaching at a local junior college, he'd jumped at the chance to supplement his income, however modestly, with a similar role for the summer.

Jerry "Fats" Lane was the Scorpions' manager. He looked the part. Closer to sixty, he wore his grizzled look like a badge of honor—and there was plenty of room for badges on the extra-large uniform jersey draped over his swollen gut. He, too, had played pro ball "back in the day," but not long or well enough to constitute a living. What he lacked in style he made up for with his keen knowledge of the game.

The first group of pitchers dug into a pail of baseballs and took their respective positions on the mounds. After a dozen warm-up tosses, they were instructed to throw a sequence of pitches as O'Toole and Lane looked on.

Like a judge at an amateur talent audition, O'Toole tolerated little mediocrity. "Number 32, you're done," he barked. "Was that really your fastball, 58?" He checked his radar gun. "Sorry, 20. Maybe next year."

I was in the final group. Almost sixty pitchers preceded me, at least fifty of whom had been summarily dismissed.

"OK, grandpa," O'Toole bellowed as I made my way to the mound. "Let's see what you've got left." It was then that he noticed my missing digit. "Wait a sec. Are you fucking kidding me?"

"Ever hear of "Three Finger" Brown?" Nick shouted from his vantage point behind the chain link fence. There was no response.

Nick shouted encouragement like a Little League parent as I tossed my allotment of warm-ups. Morbid curiosity evolved into serious interest as I ticked up the velocity.

"I'm ready," I said.

"Okay, Brown, throw me a coupl'a hard ones." So, I did.

"Shit!" O'Toole exclaimed, staring at his radar gun as if he'd been watching a porno. "Ninety-three! Who the fuck *are* you?"

I didn't respond. Instead, I tipped my glove at the catcher, signaling that a curve ball was imminent. With my newly perfected grip, the pitch broke ferociously, thoroughly handcuffing the catcher.

"What the—?" By now, both men were staring in disbelief.

"Who the heck *is* this guy?" Fats asked his pitching coach.

"Name's Brown, I think. Three Fingers Brown. Ever hear of him?"

"Yeah, idiot. He's in the Hall of Fame. Dead for half a century, at least," Fats said.

"Maybe we're in Iowa," O'Toole suggested, an oblique reference to the legendary baseball movie *Field of Dreams*. "Come 'ere, gramps."

Before long, everyone seemed to be prattling about the old guy with half a hand who threw hundred-fifty-mile-an-hour fastballs and roller-coaster curves. Suffice it to say that I made the team . . . and acquired the nickname "Four-Finger" Singer.

CHAPTER TWENTY-THREE

Kate

Jake was ecstatic when he and Nick returned from the tryouts that afternoon. He'd not only made the Scorpions' ball club, but had been named the opening day starter.

"And," Nick added, "your hot-shot husband negotiated a spectacular package of perks."

"What perks?" I asked with growing excitement.

"For starters," Jake said, "I'm excused from away games."

"Cool," I said. "What else?"

"A free pair of tickets for you and Nick behind home plate for every home game."

"*Very* cool," I said. He must be saving the best for last, I thought. "And the money?"

"Fifty," Jake said.

"Fifty grand?" My heart leapt! Nick and Jake greeted my yelp with a mutual look of amusement.

"Fifty bucks," Jake said, "per game."

"Oh." What did I know about the economics of semi-pro baseball? But I knew that Jake would have paid *them* for the privilege of playing. I couldn't have been happier—unless, of course, it *was* fifty grand.

A small but boisterous crowd braved the ninety-degree heat on opening night. Nick and I settled into our freebie seats with a pint of sun block, a gallon of water, and an ocean of anticipation.

I'd never seen Jake play ball. His career ended long before we'd met. But I'd also never seen him more radiant. There was a bounce to his step when he climbed from the dugout and strode to the mound. At first, he just stood there, savoring the moment, cupping the ball in that oily old glove like a newly hatched chick. It struck me then that baseball was as much a religion to Jake as the Good News Church had been to me—until, well . . . you know.

An eight-year-old girl sang the National Anthem. The version with the "rocking red hair" and the "lamp parts gallantly steaming." A mixture of polite applause and suppressed laughter concluded the pre-game festivities. But the umpire's scream of "Play ball!" sent shivers down my spine.

The leadoff hitter for the El Paso Diablos was a scrawny kid, barely my height. He looked even smaller, crouching in the batter's box like a cat preparing to pounce. Jake squeezed the ball in his left hand, hid it behind his back, and leaned forward for the catcher's sign. He nodded, reared back, and fired a fastball, high and tight. The kid spun away, as if ducking a right hook.

"A little chin music," laughed Nick. An attempt at intimidation, he explained, to instill fear into the hitter and throw him off stride.

Duly intimidated, the kid took Jake's next offering for a strike. He stood there motionless, the bat glued to his shoulder.

"A high fastball now, probably outside the strike zone," Nick predicted. "He'll never make contact."

Nick was right. The poor bastard swung and missed by a country mile. Jake's fourth pitch ended the drama—a curve as crooked as a pig's tail. Kid swung like he was swatting a bee, his arms extending in one direction while his butt flew in the other.

And that's how it went all night. Jake was invincible. In six shutout innings, he whiffed ten, allowing only two measly singles en route to the Scorpions' first-ever victory. Watching him pitch, it was hard to imagine he'd been away from the game for more than a decade.

While reveling in Jake's performance, I listened intently as Nick schooled me in the cat-and-mouse game between pitcher and hitter. I wasn't clueless about baseball—I had three older brothers who'd played back in Butte Rock. But Nick was a prodigy, a baseball nerd, anticipating moves, explaining strategies, and breaking down the action into nuggets of information I could easily digest.

Jake was beaming when he emerged from the clubhouse after the game. I shared his joy, but mine was tempered by guilt and shame. Jake had loved baseball long before he'd loved me. And, at least on this night, baseball had rewarded his love . . . better than I had.

A month had passed since my second encounter with Billy. Prick called the day after his visit, just as he'd threatened, and lured me to his scuzzy motel room on Miracle Mile for the payoff. The Blue Flamingo: a crumbling row of tacky motel rooms beneath a flashing neon sign. Tucked beside it was a bar with a sign reading "Girls! Girls! Girls!" I drove to that motel because I had to; no way I'd let that deadbeat into my house again.

I parked in front of Room 8, just as he'd instructed. Knocked on the beat-up metal door. The sleazeball opened it—wearing only his boxers!

"Come on in, sweetcheeks," he said.

"Fuck off," I replied. He took no offense.

"Where's the dough, darlin'?"

I handed him an envelope. It contained the $5,000 in cash I'd received for my ring, and a check in an equal amount for the rest. He peeked into the envelope while he stood there in the open door, his underwear flapping in the breeze.

"No fucking checks, Kate," he said. "I told you—cash."

There was no other way, I explained, to access the money from my bank account. "It's that or nothing," I told him. His face turned crimson. It was no longer *sweetcheeks* or *darlin'*; now he was using the c-word.

He saw that I wouldn't budge. I *couldn't* budge, so I stuck to my guns. "Tell you what," he said, calming. "Come on in for a quickie—for old times' sake—and I'll take that check of yours." He grasped my arm. I shook him loose. I was livid.

I didn't really think about the next thing I did. Did it on pure impulse. I reared back and kicked him in the balls with the force of a pile driver. As he doubled over in pain, I ran to the car, burning rubber as I sped away.

Though I'd survived the Pawn of the Ring, the guilt from my cover-up consumed me. I hated myself. And when Jake filed an insurance claim for the ring I'd supposedly lost, insurance fraud was added to my list of sins. Jake offered on several occasions to take me shopping for a replacement, but I put him off. Wearing it would be a constant reminder of my deceit and disgrace.

How had I managed to do the horrible things I'd done? Like everyone, I'd made mistakes, but mine unfailingly exploded, spewing shrapnel at bystanders like a terrorist's bomb. How could I have known that Billy would cast me as an unsuspecting participant in one of his notorious "love stories?"

Or turn up to blackmail me four years later? How could I have let myself be snookered by a man of the cloth? Does desperation breed stupidity, or is it the other way around?

I loved my husband. My infidelity was never about attraction or lust. It stemmed from frustration and yearning, in the misguided belief I could save our marriage. Instead, I nearly destroyed it. Jake's forgiveness was generous—lesser men would have abandoned me. And now, I'd rewarded his mercy by threatening our marriage yet again—withholding information that would hurt and embarrass him, and then lying to compound the problem.

I awakened each day fearful of another visit from Billy—and the consequences that would surely follow. I didn't deserve Jake . . . and he didn't deserve a royal fuck-up like me.

CHAPTER TWENTY-FOUR

Jake

I arrived at my desk on Monday morning, still basking in the glow of my triumphant return to the mound. Nothing could dampen my reverie. Or so I thought.

I began the day in the usual fashion, browsing through emails. Routine intra-office bullshit, plus a few missives from Christie on client matters. At the end of the queue was an email, with an attachment, from an "unknown sender." It's not unusual to receive a solicitation from a Nigerian attorney offering to shower you with money, if you'd simply furnish a small retainer to grease the skids; from a bank employee seeking confirmation of your social security number and password to assure your continued access to the nest egg you didn't know you had; and even a solicitation from an allegedly local girl eager to share a good time. Those are all trashed routinely. But this one was disturbingly different—it was personal and threatening.

Dear Mr. Singer:

I believe you will find the attached clip interesting, particularly in light of the young lady depicted. I would invite you to consider acquiring exclusive rights to this film. The cost is just $10,000, a price which I'm sure you'll agree is quite reasonable for such a property. Should you elect not to make this compelling investment, I will solicit your colleagues, many of whom, I'm sure, will find it irresistible. This opportunity is limited. You will be contacted for your reply in twenty-four hours.

A Close & Deeply Personal Friend of Mrs. Singer

My first thought was of Pastor Bastard. Had he the audacity to videotape his liaisons with Kate in order to blackmail us later? As outrageous as that stunt had been, it was hard to imagine he'd resort to this. I debated whether to open the attachment. The first law of email use is to trash dubious attachments. So, I wondered, do I open the attachment to assess its menace, committing a faux pas that could bring the firm to its technological knees? Or do I delete the entire message, calling Mr. Unknown Sender's bluff?

Deciding that the further spread of this potentially dangerous video was the paramount risk, I clicked on the attachment . . . and nearly fell from my chair.

I found myself watching a clip from what appeared to be a professionally produced movie—judging from the strong lighting and profusion of camera angles—in which my wife is fucked every which way by a scumbag with his hair tied up in a bun. Any doubt as to the identity of the female lead was erased with the first of countless close-ups of her shapely ass, unmistakably tattooed with that distinctive five-petaled flower. Kate was a willing participant in this fiasco, laughing, panting, and moaning in ways that were uncomfortably familiar.

I was flabbergasted . . . and madder than blazes. Mad at this brazen blackmailer, whoever the hell he was. Mad at the gods who'd allowed this abomination to disrupt my newfound reverie. But, most of all, incensed at Kate. Whatever the explanation—and I'll admit none was clearly evident at that moment—Kate had either lied or betrayed me . . . yet again.

I got up and shut the door. Painful as it was to behold, I willed myself through twenty-seven abominable minutes of agony as I searched for clues. The room in which this fiasco was filmed was too upscale to be a college dorm room and lacked the traditional appointments of a hotel room. It was devoid of photographs, posters, or artwork. It didn't look like a stage set. A bookcase hinted at a personal residence, but the camera was more focused on Kate's anatomy than on the contents of the bookshelves. Drawn curtains obscured exterior landmarks.

I'd nearly reached the end of both the film and my patience when Nick burst through the office door brandishing the sports page of the *Daily Star*. I abruptly shut down my computer.

"Hey, Ace! How's it feel to be back in the sports pages!" he beamed. His enthusiasm was tempered by the look on my face. "What's wrong, buddy?"

"Something's come up," I said. "Personal matter."

"Everyone okay?" Nick asked.

"Fine. Fine. I can't really talk about it now." I was not remotely in character and Nick knew it.

"Let me know if I can help," he said, awkwardly retreating from my office.

Still stunned, I debated my next move. I couldn't deal with anything else until I got my head around this. I arose from my desk and drove home.

Kate was in the kitchen, cleaning up the remnants of

breakfast. My entrance startled her.

"Why are you home? Did you forget something?"

"Come here," I said. "I need to show you something." Her face blanched as she walked into the living room. I showed her the email on my cellphone. Her gasp registered both horror and recognition. "Do I need to play the video?"

CHAPTER TWENTY-FIVE

Kate

"No," I said. "Please don't."

I knew this day would come. More admissions, tears, and lies to unravel. More hand-wringing, anger, disappointment. It was counterproductive, but my first instinct was to break down and cry. It's what I'd done following revelation of the Pastor Becker affair; it would be equally useless now. I covered my face with my hands. Jake's reaction was a deafening silence accompanied by a look of utter frustration and disappointment, the look a parent might give a disobedient child.

"I can explain," I said. So I did. I told him the whole rotten story, from the night in Billy's Cedar Rapids apartment to the day my friend Louise first informed me that I'd appeared on the internet. "It was the real reason I left Iowa," I admitted. I then came clean about Billy's appearance at the house, his extortion demand, and the worst part, the pawning of my engagement ring. "I didn't want you to ever see that wretched video," I told him. "It makes me look like a . . ." I couldn't say the word.

Jake fidgeted on the couch, his eyes cast downward. His look was one of sadness and defeat.

"I don't know what to say, Kate." He rubbed his temples, sighing deeply. "The explanation carries with it its own indictment. I don't know how to trust you anymore." He shrugged, looked toward the ceiling, and wrung his hands. And then he said something that stung me to my core. "I've never allowed myself to admit it until now," he said, "but my father was right."

I knew right away what he meant, what his parents thought of me. Hell, I thought it myself. Jake made the mistake of his life falling in love with me, then compounded it with marriage. We'd both made mistakes. But mine were beyond the pale.

CHAPTER TWENTY-SIX

Jake

I left the house before I could say anything else I'd regret. My marriage was a shitstorm, but before I could even think about that, I'd have to address the imminent threat posed by this lowlife, Billy Garabedian. I wasn't going to pay him, both on principle and because he'd already proven he couldn't be trusted to keep his word.

Nick was standing by the receptionist's desk when I returned to the office. "Got a minute?" I asked. He nodded, motioning me into his office.

From my behavior that morning, Nick knew something was awry. "What's the matter, Jake?"

"What would you do if someone tried to blackmail you by threatening to send your colleagues a porno flick starring your wife?"

He glared at me in disbelief. "You're kidding, right?"

"Wrong."

I related the circumstances, as described by Kate, that had given rise to the video, as well as the details of Garabedian's initial extortion. I then showed Nick the email on my cell phone—sans the movie.

"Seems to me that most of the damage has already been done," Nick concluded. "And if he's already blackmailed Kate and broken his commitment, it wouldn't make sense to pay him again," he added, shaking his head. "I'd try to nail the bastard."

"I agree."

"I know a Detective Lieutenant on the police force," he said. "Vito Vitale. My Dad and I used him as an expert witness on a criminal matter. Got a nice payday, so he owes me."

"Is he discreet?"

"Discreet *and* savvy," Nick assured me, "but . . ."

"But what?"

"His personal hygiene will make you cringe."

Two hours later I found myself in the presence of the aforementioned Detective Lt. Vitale. His office smelled like a locker room.

"What can I do for you?" he asked. He was a prodigious man, an oversized pear with a grapefruit head and a moustache reminiscent of Agatha Christie's Detective Poirot.

I showed him both the offending email and enough of the video to both titillate and inform him. "Hmmm," he said, stroking his chin, "this guy's an idiot. He's exposed himself completely, and he's relying solely on your fear of embarrassment to seal the deal." He leaned back in his chair, dangerously approaching the tipping point. As the springs groaned, I pictured him crashing to the floor like a latter-day Humpty Dumpty. "Tell ya what we're gonna do," he said, his eyes narrowing. "When this bozo calls, you agree to meet him with the money, but *you* establish the meeting place: the courtyard next to the art museum downtown—it's nearby and public, and it's got good sight lines and limited points of egress. He'll resist at first, but you'll play his bluff. Then he'll agree—he has to. Sending the video to others won't net him a dime—and it'll eliminate the leverage he thinks he's got."

He laid out the remaining details of the proposed sting like a movie director briefing his cast for a shoot. I'd wear a wire and he'd videotape the entire proceeding from a safe distance. "Kind of *tit*-for-tat, don't you think?" he quipped, scratching his left armpit while cackling at his wordplay.

Billy called the next day to seal the deal: a $10,000 "investment" in what he called his "Kate Love Story." I agreed to the payment.

"You'll be happy you did," he said.

"I have conditions," I said. I was going off-script.

"No conditions," he replied.

"No payment," I responded.

"What conditions?"

"We do this like it's a real business transaction . . . instead of extortion," I said. "You sign a piece of paper. It says you're selling me exclusive rights to the video in all forms, and any other photos or videos of Kate, in exchange for a one-time payment of $10,000. I hand you an envelope with ten grand in cash. And then I never see your face again." This, I thought, might induce him to drop his guard and, if the police proved ineffective, give me some leverage against him in the future should evidence of the video resurface.

Billy was silent for several moments. I could almost hear the wheels grinding in that pumpkin head of his.

"I'll call you back."

"No, you won't!" I shouted into the receiver. "It's take it or leave it. Right now! If you weren't such a dickhead, you'd realize I'm legitimizing what would otherwise be a criminal act. I'm protected and you're protected," I fibbed.

"Fine," he said. Billy wasn't the brightest bulb in the box.

"Tomorrow. Eleven A.M. In the courtyard of the art museum downtown." I hung up before he could object.

Moments later I called Detective Lt. Vitale, confirming the rendezvous.

I sat alone on a bench, wearing a wire, in the museum courtyard at the appointed time. Detective Lt. Vitale stood just inside the museum entrance, with a hand-held videotape camera, his prodigious profile obscured by tinted glass. Two plainclothes officers, camouflaged as panhandlers, idled separately nearby, each in radio contact with the detective and each other.

Although Garabedian didn't show up until 12:15, he'd been spotted by the undercover officers fifteen minutes earlier, surveying the area for signs of an ambush, too dense to identify the officers as a threat. Satisfied that his mark was present and his payday assured, Billy strolled arrogantly into the courtyard toward the bench where I sat.

"You're late." I said.

"Fuck you," he snapped as he sat down beside me. "Where's my money?"

I withdrew an envelope containing the cash.

"Let me see it." I opened it, flashing its contents. I withdrew it as he thrust out his hand, returning it to my jacket pocket.

"Okay, now, let's get this clear," I said, glaring at him. "In exchange for this ten grand payment, you agree you'll never circulate the video of you fucking my wife, or any other photos or videos of my wife, anywhere ever again. I'm paying you to keep this out of circulation *permanently*, you got that?"

"Sure, I'm a filmmaker and you're buying my movie," he sniggered. "You said you'd write it up in an agreement, all legal and all."

"You're a criminal, Billy, not an entrepreneur."

"Whatever floats your boat, big fella."

From my other pocket, I withdrew a single sheet of paper, thrusting it at Billy. He snatched it with a smirk, unfolded it, and began to read.

I'd kept it simple. He'd acknowledge in the document that he made the film and was offering it to me for $10,000 in cash; I'd agree to the purchase of all rights to the video, and anything else portraying Kate, in exchange for the payment. He retained no rights whatsoever. "There's nothing here tying you to the email you sent me yesterday, in which you threatened to pass on this film to my colleagues if I failed to pay up," I said. "But I need to hear you say it, clearly and unequivocally: that if I pay you this money, *nothing* portraying Kate will ever again see the light of day."

He gave me a smug grin. "I won't do what I said in the email," he muttered. "Fucking promise."

Almost, but not quite. I needed to eliminate all doubt. I reached back into my pocket for the envelope containing the payoff. "And if I don't invest," I said, waving the envelope in his face, "you'll do what?"

Billy was getting annoyed. "I'll share your wife's ass with the whole fucking world!" he seethed. "Now give me my fucking money!"

He put his grubby hand on the envelope containing the cash. We clutched it simultaneously, until he signed the paper with his free hand and the pen I'd provided, at which point I released my grip. A nasty grin spread across his stubbly face . . . but quickly evaporated as Detective Lt. Vitale and his colleagues converged upon the courtyard from three directions.

"You fucking—" he bellowed, turning to flee. I sprang up and tackled him with special gusto just as the officers arrived.

"Jig's up," I clucked. I'd always wanted to say that.

CHAPTER TWENTY-SEVEN

Kate

Two days later, while Jake was at work, I left. Or, at least I tried to. We'd barely spoken since he'd confronted me about the video. I needed to give him his space . . . and time to decide if he wanted anything more to do with me.

The video had shocked him. Even though he understood it had happened long ago and that I'd been tricked, it wasn't like watching a piano recital. It was graphic, and I'd submitted willingly to the acts, if not their recording. It looked—and I felt—like I was as depraved as Billy. I wasn't the woman he thought he'd married. I never had been.

Sitting home alone for those two days was torture. I agonized over what to do. I figured I'd pretty much used up all my mulligans with Jake. How many times can you screw up this badly and expect a reprieve? I realized I needed to leave, but for how long, where to, and to what end? Jake told me they'd arrested Billy, and that he'd signed some contract, but I knew, somehow, I'd never be free of him. I'd always wonder whether or when he'd reappear, shattering my world all over again.

For lack of a better alternative, I decided to return to Iowa. I'd tell my parents about the entire episode—so their lack of knowledge could never again be used against me. They, too, would be shocked and disappointed, but they'd get over it—I was still, after all, their only daughter. But I'd draw the line at my infidelity with the pastor—that would be too much for them to accept.

I left a note for Jake on the kitchen table. It took all morning to write.

> Dearest Jake:
>
> I think it's time for me to leave. My transgressions seem like an endless stream of insults. I can't keep hurting you like this.
>
> I knew, from the very beginning, that we didn't belong together. I told you as much after that awful dinner at Jeremy's. Your father warned you, too. You thought you'd mold me into someone better than I am. But you couldn't. I'm ashamed of what I am, what I've probably always been, and I can't keep embarrassing and disappointing you. You deserve so much more.
>
> I'm going to visit my parents in Iowa. I have no idea for how long. It will give us both time to think. In the meantime, do whatever you feel you must; I won't stand in your way.
>
> All my love, Kate

I filled the trunk with suitcases—clothes and toiletries to last at least a month. I didn't really have a plan, but sitting alone at home, feeling sorry for myself, was no longer an option.

I don't know why I did what I did next. In retrospect, it

seems rather silly. I was all set to go when it occurred to me that I hadn't shopped for groceries in days. I'd been too self-absorbed. The refrigerator was nearly empty. I couldn't leave Jake like that. So, I added a little "P.S." to the end of my note, in anticipation of a last-minute grocery run: *There's some leftover eggplant in the fridge. Bought a few things to hold you over for a few more days. I love you.*

I drove to Rincon Market on Sixth. The lot was full, so I parked across the street. I bought Jake the things he liked best—and a few organic items that were good for him, things he didn't always have the good sense to eat without a nudge from me.

"Are you okay?" asked the checkout girl at the register when she saw me crying.

"Fine," I said.

"Can I help you with that?" asked the bagger. My cloth sack was nearly overflowing.

"No thanks," I said.

It was my last conversation.

My eyes were moist and blurry as I walked to the curb. I wondered what Jake would think when he arrived home to an empty house and my farewell note. Would my departure bring him anger or relief? My mind wandered as I stepped over the curb and into the street. When I looked up, my eye caught the outline of a big white truck barreling toward me.

For that first split second, I was paralyzed with fear. But then, a strange sensation overcame me. The wild roar of the oncoming truck offered a release from the sadness, self-loathing, and indecision that crippled me.

I embraced that truck like the child I'd always longed for. I shifted the bag of groceries into my left arm and braced for impact. It was over. Or so I thought.

CHAPTER TWENTY-EIGHT

Jake

The call came from Detective Lt. Vitale. He'd been among the first to arrive at the scene. I assumed, of course, he was calling about Billy.

"Mr. Singer, uh, Jake," he stammered. I sensed something was terribly wrong. "I'm sorry to inform you," he said, "that your wife's been involved in an accident." He snorted, then paused. The silence was deafening. "I'm sorry to say that she didn't make it."

I could scarcely comprehend what he'd told me. I felt dizzy, nauseated. How was this possible? So much had happened over these last few months, so much to process, and now the unimaginable. "How?"

"Hit and run. She was crossing the street at Rincon Market on Sixth."

"I . . . uh . . . where is she now?"

"City morgue." He gave me the address.

Christie was about to enter my office as I hung up the phone.

"Jake, you're white as a ghost! What's wrong?"

"It's Kate. She's . . . she's been in an accident."

Reading the grief in my eyes, Christie lurched forward, ostensibly to embrace me, but restrained herself, seemingly reluctant to do anything that could be misconstrued. "How is she?"

"She's dead, Christie." I could barely articulate the words.

She gasped. Dispensing with protocol, she hugged me tightly.

From his secretary's desk just down the hallway from my office, Nick caught our embrace. The gesture telegraphed horror, not affection. Concerned, he rushed down the hall and into my office. "What's happened?"

"It's Kate," Christie said, while I slumped into my chair, mute, my head in my hands. "An accident." She shook her head to convey the gravity of the event.

"Jesus! Jake!" It was all he could say.

Christie took charge of my client matters, while Nick drove me to the morgue. My initial shock evolved into numbness, a self-induced narcotic to ward off an emotional cocktail of heartbreak, anger, and guilt. It was as if Kate had dropped a final bombshell upon the crumbling ruins of our marriage. Part of me felt relief, realizing that she'd spared me from the quandary of choosing between the repudiation or reclamation of our relationship; part of me felt guilt, for offering her no quarter in the wake of the latest debacle. But when they led us into that cold, sterile room and unveiled her lifeless, battered body, I was overwhelmed by a precarious mixture of love, regret, and pity, like dissonant chords from an untuned instrument.

Like mine, Kate's wounds were fresh and raw. No longer could I see that perky, winsome girl I'd met that day in Cambridge, the quirky waif who'd charmed me and captured my heart. Instead, I saw a troubled soul, snake-bitten, haunted by unfortunate choices, a wife who'd deceived me and broken my heart.

Detective Lt. Vitale arrived moments later, clumsily expressing his condolences as he mined earwax crudely from his left ear with his index finger. There were no leads yet on the driver who'd hit her, he reported. "It's strange," he said. "Witnesses said she froze. Made no effort to get out of the way." He parted his lips to say more, hesitating briefly before continuing. "Where was she going?"

"What do you mean?"

"The trunk of her vehicle was filled with suitcases."

That was news to me. "She didn't say anything to me," I told him, conceding that things had been awkward between us since the blackmail episode.

"I see." Vitale eyed me curiously.

"Another thing I don't quite get," he said, scratching at the stubble on his cheek. "She was carrying a sack full of groceries. Why would she do that if she was leaving home?"

"Guess it depends on where she was going," Nick suggested.

"Hmmm." He swiped his index finger casually across his greasy moustache.

"Why is this relevant, Vito?" Nick asked. "This was an accident, right?"

"Yup, far as I can tell. Just tying up some loose ends." He turned to me. "Jake, for the record, is this the body of your wife, Kate Singer?"

I took one final glance. "Yes," I acknowledged, imparting a certain reality to what, to that point, had seemed impossibly surreal.

Nick drove me home, coming inside to keep me company. Kate's note awaited us on the kitchen table. I bit my lip as I read it, then handed it to Nick without comment.

"That explains the suitcases," Nick said.

"I need a beer. Want one?" Nick shook his head. I got up from the table and opened the refrigerator, snatching a Sam

Adams from the top shelf. The fridge was nearly empty. "And this explains her trip to the market," I said, shaking my head. "She just never made it back."

Nick was solicitous and patient. He was well aware of the anguish I'd endured with Kate. My largely unemotional response to this latest blow perplexed him. "Talk to me, Jake."

"What's there to say? I feel everything at once. She was distressed enough to leave. Did some part of her decide at the last second to hold her ground as the truck approached?"

"If she planned on killing herself, she would have written a suicide note," Nick said.

"First two paragraphs read like one."

"Hell, she went shopping for you, Jake."

"Jesus, Nick, I don't know what the hell to think!" Nor how to grieve.

Nick remained for several hours. He urged me to join him and Trudy for dinner at their place. I thanked him, but declined. I needed some time alone.

There's a tavern near our home—*my* home now. Skip's. I'd been there once before, with Nick, after a University of Arizona baseball game. It's as vapid as a local bar can be, the epitome of a dive bar, but with edible food. Recalling that my car remained at the office, I walked the five blocks, hoping it would help me sort my emotions. It didn't, and I now regretted being alone.

I took up a spot at the bar and ordered a beer. A few stools to my right sat a heavy-set guy in his mid-thirties, hunched over a pint. He wore an olive drab tee shirt and military camouflage pants. He offered a perfunctory nod as I sat down. I returned the gesture. By all appearances, he'd been there a while.

I had little appetite, but ordered a burger, if only to dull the effect of the alcohol, which I was consuming as if racing the cut-off for happy hour. The bartender watched me warily, aware that my drinking was a tad too intense and purposeful. After a while, he leaned over the bar to address me.

"You okay, pal?" he inquired with what seemed like genuine concern. He was tall and bespectacled, a twenty-something with a ponytail and tattoos as dense as legal disclaimers.

"Tough day," I said.

"Tell me about it!" barked the burly guy on my right, later introduced to me as Benny. "My fat fucking wife's balling some other dude," he groused. "Quit her job, hangs around the house all day watching soaps while I work overtime to cover the rent."

"I can relate to parts of that," I muttered.

"Which parts?"

"The fucking part and the quit-her-job part."

"Bummer," Benny said. "Well, at least she's not loungin' around watchin' the soaps."

"Not any more," I said. "Got hit by a truck today."

Benny nearly dropped his stein. "Jesus, man! She okay?"

"Dead."

"Fuckin' A!"

The conversation devolved into a cross between a therapy session and a wake. Benny and I traded stories of misfortune while draining the tap. He'd served in Iraq, he said, coming home with little more than "an honorable discharge, a handshake, and PTSD." At his urging, I related the saga of my missing finger and my reinvigorated baseball career.

"So, you're that 'Four-Finger Singer' dude I read about in the papers last week?"

"Yeah, that's me." It was the one high point in the

depressing landscape of my shattered life.

By now, most of the bar's regulars had gathered around me, simultaneously fascinated and horrified by my story. Encouraged by alcohol and the anonymity of my audience, I held nothing back. I described Kate's infidelity with the man I called Pastor Bastard, told them about the pornographic movie in which she'd unwittingly starred, and about the blackmail efforts and arrest of its producer/co-star. Benny told of the horrors he'd seen in Iraq, trembling as he recounted how his buddy had been literally torn asunder by an IED as he stood helplessly by. Pedro, a truck driver, described his early years in the barrios of Mexico City, and the sacrifices his mother made for her seven children in the absence of their drug-addicted father. Ted, the bartender, shared the promise of his college years, his dream to be a writer, and the impact of persistent rejection upon his psyche, confidence, and personal relationships. Unexpectedly, this recital of woes from ordinary joes buoyed my sagging spirit at the moment I needed it most. Benny even offered to preside over my poor wife's funeral.

I'd had an abominable day capping a horrific week. But, as my new acquaintances could testify, we all had our crosses to bear. I had earned those few hours of dissipation. But I didn't want to find myself in Skip's a year later, bemoaning my fate in an alcohol-induced fog. I may not have mastered my grief on that barstool, but I resolved to look forward, rather than back. I had to get on with my life.

PART TWO

The Curious State of the Late, Great Kate

CHAPTER TWENTY-NINE

Jake

As word of my widowhood spreads, women emerge from the woodwork, marking their territory with casseroles. Tuna noodle, chicken fajita, and hamburger casseroles arrive on my doorstep like junk mail, borne by females of every size and shape, all curiously unattached, lavishly coiffed, and more provocatively dressed than the occasion requires. They tender their culinary concoctions like tickets, hoping to secure admission to the home of this young, grieving widower, angling for a proffered cup of coffee or, even better, a glass of wine.

Ladies from the Good News Church, none of whom I'd ever met, deliver their favorite dishes, in rotation, on Mondays, Wednesdays, and Fridays. Lorna O'Malley, my newly divorced next-door neighbor, contributes on Sundays and Tuesdays. She hugs her casserole like a football as she prances across the yard, evading the clutches of her four children like a halfback piercing a line of defenders. I eat what I can, but with enough food for a regiment, the garbage disposal gorges to the brink of indigestion.

Returning to work is uncomfortable. To all but Nick and Christie, who know of the tribulations preceding Kate's death, my bizarre behavior at the funeral is incomprehensible. Condolences are awkward, tinged with pity and disapproval.

I've breached the etiquette of widowhood in every possible fashion, from my dry-eyed grieving to my baffling attack on poor Pastor Bastard. Going to work on the day after burying my wife seems cold-hearted to some, but I've no desire to shuffle around an empty house, struggling to unravel my muddled emotions.

While Nick is supportive and reassuring, Christie is clearly at sea. As much as she longs to confer comfort, she's wary of crossing the hazy line between sympathy and impropriety. The ground rules we laid in Flagstaff made no provision for circumstances like these. Naturally cautious and sensitive to appearances, she reins herself in, even as I crave her comfort.

To avoid the appearance of callousness, I skip the Scorpions' games on the weekend after the funeral. It's a hard choice: there's nothing I'd rather do than escape to the mound, a place where the turmoil of my suddenly altered life might be eclipsed, if even for a few brief hours, by the soothing rhythms of baseball.

I adjust to that altered life like a driver in stop-and-go traffic. There are nights I awaken with a start. I roll to my right, expecting to feel the warmth of Kate's body, to hear the gentle cadence of her breathing. And then, abruptly, silence and emptiness dash my reverie, cruelly reopening the wounds of my widowhood.

The onslaught of casseroles eventually subsides. Their makers, content to have entered and planted a seed, serially reclaim their empty Pyrex ovenware and ceramic casserole dishes. They mark their calendars with reminders to reestablish contact with the hunky widower after a suitable period of mourning has passed. What constitutes a suitable period varies among the suitors—six months for the more timid of the lot; three, perhaps, for the more daring. But for Lorna O'Malley, my zealous neighbor, there's no time like the present.

Lorna's ex-husband, Randy, is a brash and presumptuous real estate agent, the kind who plasters his face everywhere—on billboards, buses, newspapers, magazines, and, evidently, between the legs of his curvaceous young assistant. Lorna, who'd been screwed by the bastard with sufficient frequency to produce four offspring in the first four years of their eight-year marriage, forgave him his indiscretion—until her discovery of the half-dozen or more that preceded it. She's been divorced for nearly a year.

It's Saturday afternoon, a week since the funeral. As I sit alone, feeling sorry for myself, Lorna calls. She graciously offers to relieve me of the burden of preparing dinner. The kids are with their dastardly father, she reveals, and she's bought a rib eye too big to consume alone. Would I care to join her?

I hesitate momentarily, but the thought of a home-cooked steak dinner is too good to resist. "Sure," I say, "I'll bring the wine."

Lorna O'Malley is, by any measure, a very attractive woman. Tall, even statuesque, she's a miracle of Technicolor, with emerald-green eyes that play off a luscious mane of shimmering red hair. Even after the birth of four children, her figure is undiminished.

When I arrive on her doorstep, I sense an agenda. She wears a deeply scooped white silk blouse over a lacy, peek-a-boo black bra, and jeans that hug her hips like shrink-wrap. Her elaborate preparations—three plates of hors d'oeuvres plus a cheese plate, not to mention two kinds of appetizers, belies her commitment to a "no-fuss, casual" supper.

"Glad I caught you," she says. "I thought you might like a change from that parade of casseroles."

"You've gone to a lot of trouble," I say.

"Not at all," she lies with a demure smile. She motions toward the bottle of Malbec I clutch in my mangled left hand. "Would you like to open that?"

The kitchen looks like the staging area for a wedding banquet. She hands me a corkscrew. "Screw cap," I note, having already opened it.

Lorna engages in mindless small talk, fussing with preparations as I observe from a barstool at the kitchen counter. Barely thirty, she's endured more than she'd bargained for with her humiliating marriage and hasty motherhood.

"Randy came from a big, Irish-Catholic family," she explains. "He'd have kept me pumping out kids till I'd worn out my girl parts. Had my tubes tied after the fourth," she says. I cringe at the torrent of unsolicited information.

Lorna consumes the Malbec with urgency. Before long, she withdraws from her well-stocked wine rack another bottle, which I warily uncork. She's buzzing when she extracts the steak from the broiler, plating it breathlessly alongside generous helpings of green beans almondine and fingerling potatoes. When we shift to the dining room, the conversation grows more discomfiting.

"I can't imagine how you're dealing with the shock of Kate's passing," she says.

"It hasn't been easy," I acknowledge, hoping to seal off that particular line of inquiry. "But you've got your own challenges," I add, sawing through my overcooked steak, "coping with four kids all by yourself. How do you manage?"

"Here's how," she says, her voice rising, as she pours herself another glass of wine. "It's brutal. They take every *fucking* ounce of my strength." Realizing I've struck a nerve, I try to shift gears. "This steak is—"

"When fucking Randy takes them—he's supposed to take them on weekends—I'm too tired to do anything but sleep. And half the time he fucks up and bails, leaving me with another couple days of hell." She drains her glass, barely touching her steak. "I long to have a life, Jake, you know? To get out of this goddamn house once in a while!" She refills her glass and guzzles it. "I'm lonely. I shouldn't admit it, but I am."

Lorna begins to weep. I panic. "Listen, Lorna, maybe I should head on back—"

"No, Jake, *please* stay. I'm sorry. It's just a little bit . . . overwhelming . . . sometimes. I need a man I can count on. But what man in his right mind would want me?" she sniffles. "I'm an emotional and physical wreck!"

"You're anything but," I assure her, hoping to avert an impending meltdown. My troubles seem to pale by comparison. "You're a beautiful woman, Lorna. You're still young, totally desirable, and—"

"And toting around f-f-four f-f-fucking kids!" She slurs her words while dividing the last of the wine between her glass and the tablecloth.

I decide to take action. Lorna's completely unhinged. Her mascara dissolves into inky streams that dribble down her rouged cheeks. I feel partially responsible for her plight; I should have monitored her intake or, at the very least, consumed more of the wine myself. When she rises from the table, I do the same, lunging to support her as she staggers.

"Listen, I'll clean up here," I say. "Why don't you lie down for a while?" She nods reluctantly as I brace her. She points me in the direction of the bedroom. With one arm around her back and the other beneath her shoulder, I guide her into the bedroom, turn on the light, and lay her gently on the bedspread. She moans softly. Within moments, she's asleep.

I return to the dining room, collect the dishes, retrieve the leftovers. I place the dirty dishes in the dishwasher, locate the soap, and run the machine. I check on Lorna. Out like a light. I debate the merits of partially undressing her for bed, deciding the notion is too fraught with danger; besides, it would take a crowbar to loosen those jeans. I lock the front door behind me and return to my own house of misery.

At ten the next morning, the doorbell rings. I spot Lorna through the sidelight. She sees me, too, so I can hardly evade her. With trepidation, I open the door.

"Hi," she says. A weak smile registers her embarrassment.

"Hi."

"Can I come in?"

"Of course." She looks far better than she did when I left her. "You clean up nicely," I quip, as we stand awkwardly in the foyer.

"Speaking of which, thank you, Jake. You didn't have to clean the place up." She smiles. "I want to apologize for my behavior. I'm thoroughly embarrassed."

"No need to apologize, Lorna."

Against my better judgment, I offer her some coffee, having made a fresh pot. We walk to the kitchen. I pour her a cup and reclaim my own. We sit across from one another at the kitchen table. I'm struck, as she slowly sips her coffee, at how radiantly beautiful she is.

"It's been a hard year," she says, her palms pressed tightly around her coffee cup. "I'm sorry I chose to unburden myself on you—you've had enough of your own misfortune." She looks up. "And just to correct any misimpression, I love my children dearly."

"It's all right, Lorna. Sometimes you just need someone to talk to."

"Jake," she says, "I have a confession." She strokes her cup, pondering her next words. "I'd foolishly hoped for something more last night," she says, "something I had no right to seek from you, especially now." Lorna raises the cup to her lips, taking a healthy gulp. She lifts her gaze across the table and into my eyes. Hers are moistening, but she maintains her composure. "Would you mind . . ." she asks, haltingly, "just holding me . . . for a few moments?"

By now, I've let down my defenses completely. We're two lost souls, in pain, equally in need of comfort. "Happy to," I say, rising to approach her, grasping her hand, guiding her up from her chair. I enclose her gently in my arms. She shudders in my embrace; I squeeze her more tightly. It feels liberating.

Moments pass. We break from our embrace. Our eyes meet. We kiss. As one thing leads inevitably to another, the venue shifts from kitchen to bedroom, where we make rejuvenating love. And, for an hour or so, each of us is infinitely happier than either has been in a very long time.

CHAPTER THIRTY

Kate

Okay, I'm dead. I get that. But I don't know the rules. It's like playing a video game without instructions. I push the imaginary buttons to see what happens. Discoveries abound.

I find, for example, that by concentrating on a destination, I can transport myself wherever I choose. Who'd have guessed the dead would be equipped with GPS?

What I discover next is even more incredible.

On the Monday after my funeral, I find myself in the center of Tucson, on the plaza by the city's main library. Occupying a corner of the plaza is a pack of those brazen, tattoo-smothered bicycle messengers who delight in terrorizing motorists and pedestrians. One of the youngest, his arms teeming with more characters than a Chinese take-out menu, devours a sandwich. The more I focus on him, the more I connect with his thoughts and emotions. He steals glances at a young female counterpart; I peg her as a recent addition. He longs to ask her out, but hesitates for fear of rejection. Men are such idiots sometimes! The girl sits quietly, perhaps ten feet away, pecking at her wilted salad. Every now and then, she sneaks a peek at the kid.

And then, the most amazing thing! While the bashful mating dance continues, I form words in my mind, as if speaking to the kid directly: "Ask her out already, you idiot!" I say. Chinese Menu Man turns, searching for the source of the voice in his head. "I'm right behind you," I say, forgetting that I have less physical presence than his breath. He pivots again, a baffled look on his face.

"Was that you?" he asks a companion.

"Was *what* me?"

I concentrate now on the girl. She's aching for the kid's attention.

"She wants you to ask her out," I tell Menu Man. "So, do it!" The kid puts down his sandwich, shakes his head, approaches the young lady, and scores a date.

Encouraged by my swelling tally of talents, I decide to visit Jake's office. I concentrate on my destination, but my GPS falters. I land on the second level of a parking garage two blocks away. Shit! Lacking a body, I can't 'walk' even a millimeter. I try again, focusing harder.

Bingo! I'm in Christie Loring's office. My goodness, she *is* a lovely girl. I'd forgotten that she's actually several years older than I am—or was. I watch her closely as she pecks away at her keyboard, stopping every now and then to consult the notes she's scribbled on a legal pad. I try to penetrate her thoughts, but reap just a dizzying tangle of "theretos," "whereases" and other legal gobbledygook. She sighs deeply, reciting to herself something called a severability clause. "If any provision herein, or any portion thereof, is rendered invalid by operation of law, judgment, or court order, the remaining provisions and/or portions thereof shall remain valid and enforceable." Wow! This is how Jake makes his living? Boring people to death? At last, Christie sits back and taps the 'print' button, unleashing a flood of paper from a nearby printer.

Christie gathers the printed pages and returns to her desk.

She thinks about Jake. And not the way I've imagined. No, she isn't plotting to jump his suddenly widowed bones, debating how long to wait before pouncing. She's hurting inside, afraid to express her sympathy for fear of violating some unwritten rules of conduct. Her adoration for my husband is as pure as a symphony. She wants to comfort him, not sleep with him—at least for now.

Have I been wrong all along? I'll take it under advisement, as Jake would say.

CHAPTER THIRTY-ONE

Jake

Two weeks after the funeral, I suit up for my second start for the Scorpions. I'm eager to return to the mound. Nick sits in the stands behind home plate, his wife, Trudy, beside him, in the seat intended for Kate. Behind the home dugout, three rows up, sits Lorna O'Malley, applauding my every pitch like a smitten cheerleader.

I haven't touched a baseball in two weeks. I fear there'll be rust from the layoff. The crowd buzzes as I take my place on the hill. Anyone previously unaware that Four-Finger Singer had tragically lost his wife in an accident would certainly know by now. The grizzled sports editor for the *Daily Star* sits in the front row behind the Scorpions' dugout, itching to write a hokey story about the mourning, digit-challenged left-hander who overcomes his grief to spin a gem for the home team.

It isn't meant to be—or so it appears as I throw my first pitch, a mediocre fastball, eminently hittable. I struggle to keep my curve out of the dirt. My mind wanders. I think of Kate, Lorna, Christie. My emotions ricochet like the silver ball in a pinball machine: from sadness to anger to guilt, and back again. I surrender a run in the first inning, another in the second. My confidence wilts.

We trail by two as I take the mound in the third. I walk the first batter on four pitches. None is remotely near the plate.

Fats Lane springs from the Scorpions' dugout. I stomp around the mound as he calls time and waddles in my direction.

"What the fuck, Jake?" he says. Not the pep talk I anticipated. "I know you've been through a lot lately, but this is *baseball*."

"Must've made a wrong turn," I say. "Meant to attend the opera."

"Jesus Christ, Singer! Look, what I'm tryin' to tell you is that this is the place you can fucking forget about all that shit." Sensitivity is not his forte. "That stuff just don't matter here. Let it go. Fuck that shit and pitch like I know you can, okay?" He trains his bloodshot eyes on mine while the home plate umpire saunters to the mound to break up our conference. Lane turns, reprising his waddle back to the dugout.

Lane is a psychological genius. It's as if he's pushed some reset button in my brain. Suddenly, I'm myself again, striking out two of the next three batters and seven of the next nine. According to the radar gun, I've added five miles-per-hour to my fastball. My curve is breaking like nobody's business.

In the seventh, the Scorpions parlay four hits into a couple of runs to tie the score, and add the go-ahead run in the eighth.

"Wanna pitch the ninth?" Fats asks me from the dugout after we've taken the lead. "Or are you late for the fucking opera?"

"Ain't no fat lady singing tonight!" I bellow. I love how baseball shatters the rules of logic and grammar.

Nick and Trudy shout their encouragement from behind home plate. And in spite of the noisy crowd, I can hear the yelps of excitement emanating from the stunning redhead in the third row.

In the ninth, I allow a leadoff single. Fats hovers over the dugout steps, ready to pounce. I stare him down before fanning the next three hitters on nine straight strikes to seal the victory.

CHAPTER THIRTY-TWO

Kate

I wouldn't have missed it for the world. But I almost do. Once again, I've teleported myself to a parking lot. At least it's the ballpark parking lot. Narrowing my focus, I inch closer. My next-to-last stop is the ballpark men's room. How do these guys put up with such filth?

I finally get there, right where I'd be sitting—if I still had an ass to sit on. Immediately, I lock in on Nick. I'm fascinated by his knowledge of the game. Just as he schooled me during Jake's first outing about the mental battle between hitter and pitcher, he blathers to Trudy about strategies and pitch selection. Trudy couldn't give a shit, but I do. I listen carefully, hoping to absorb as much as I can.

"Who's he keep looking at?" Trudy asks Nick at the start of the third inning. As he struggles on the mound, Jake casts repeated glances into the crowd.

"What do you mean?"

"He keeps looking into the stands behind the dugout."

"What makes you think he's looking at someone in particular?"

"I don't know," Trudy says, "but watch him."

So, naturally, *I* watch him. Like a hawk. And I peel my eyes—figuratively speaking, of course—on the area Trudy points out. I immediately notice the hot redhead in the third row. Lorna

O'Malley. Not possible, I'm thinking, but it's plain as day.

"Look, Nick," Trudy says, as Jake leaves the mound at the end of the third. "Who's he smiling at?"

Well, Nick surely doesn't know Lorna O'Malley, and I rather hope he never will. But *I* have my work cut out for me.

I make my way to Jake's house (formerly *Kate* and Jake's house) later that evening. Takes me two tries. First one lands me in the backyard pool.

My worst fears are realized. There they are, Jake and Red, sharing a pizza in *my* living room.

"Whoa, enough wine, Lorna! Remember what happened the last time," Jake says. As Red laughs, I shudder to think what happened the last time.

"Won't do that to you again," she says. "Promise." *Hmmm.*

I try to pry into Jake's head, but with limited success. Maybe I'm not supposed to know what he's thinking. Or maybe he's just too complicated. They didn't call him Einstein for nothing. But one thing is certain—Jake looks mighty comfortable with Mother Hubbard in my living room.

And, it turns out, in my bedroom, too! Jesus Christ, Jake, must you? I've only been gone two weeks, for heaven's sake!

Okay, I know, I railed against what Billy had done to me, filming me in supposedly private moments for others to watch. Now, I'm one of the very voyeurs I claim to detest. Sorry, but I'm just too ticked off to leave.

The lights go out. At least Billy's not filming. And the dark's no obstacle to the dead. So I watch like a rubbernecker passing a car wreck. Jesus, Red, no wonder you've had four kids in four years! Relentless! And Jake, where the hell did you learn *that*?

Finally, I can't take it any longer. "Stop!" I cry out. "Fucking stop!"

Jake withdraws like his mother just caught him masturbating. "What'd I do?" he asks Red.

"What are you talking about?" Red says, a look of surprise on her face that Jake can't see.

"You asked me to stop!"

"I did no such thing!"

"You yelled 'stop . . . fucking stop'!" *Ha! I'm on his wave length!*

Red lifts herself off her back and reaches out to where she thinks a lamp switch might be. Jake leans over her, switching the light on. "What's wrong, Jake?"

Jake shakes his head, wondering if he's imagined it. On second thought, the voice is familiar to him. *Getting warmer, Jake!*

"Okay, must be my imagination playing tricks," he says. "Let's just pick up where we left off."

No, Jake, that's not where you left off! His mouth's heading south! Really, Jake?

"Her pubic hair's not even red!" I bark. "She's a fake redhead!"

"What the fuck!" Jake is now thoroughly blown away. He recognizes the voice. "She's in my fucking head!"

Lorna's had enough. Jake's not himself tonight, she concludes. "How much did you drink?" she asks him.

"Look, Lorna, I'm really sorry. I think I'm having an attack of the guilts. Maybe it's too soon. It was wonderful the last time, but maybe I'm not ready to turn this into a relationship . . . at least not yet." *The last time?*

I decide to drill more deeply into the mind of poor Lorna as she lies spread-eagled on my bed. *This is just too weird*, she thinks. "It's okay, Jake," she says. "I get it. It's too much, too soon." She gets up and begins to dress. Jake, completely dazed, says nothing. "I'll find my way out," Fake Red says, leaving the room.

Jake grabs a robe and sits on the bed, a look of terror plastered across his big mug. He looks like I must have looked when I saw that bastard trucker bearing down on me.

"Tell me I imagined that, Kate," he says. The last thing he wants is an answer from me. I hesitate for a moment, wondering whether to come clean, recalling that my failure to do so in the past was what torpedoed our marriage.

"Sorry, Jake. You didn't imagine it." I watch him shiver.

"I can't really fathom this, Kate." He remains on the bed, pressing his fingers into his forehead. "You've gotta help me here."

"Okay," I say. "But I haven't got many more answers than you do."

Jake sighs deeply. He's flabbergasted. I proceed to explain what little I've deduced about my curious existence, my presence at the funeral, my developing ability to read minds, to travel, and communicate telepathically.

"You were only in *my* head?" he asks, fidgeting. "That's why Lorna couldn't hear you?"

"Apparently."

"Are you here to haunt me or to punish me?" Now he's irritated. Hey, it isn't every day you talk to your dead wife—and she responds.

"Are those my only choices? No, Jake. I love you."

"You're jealous? Is that why you dropped a bomb on my night with Lorna?"

"Maybe a little," I concede, "but no, that's not why. She's no better for you than I was."

Jake springs from the bed. "Who are you to say?" He's angry now.

"Look, Jake, you don't always make the wisest decisions about women. Consider me, for example."

"So why are you here, dammit?"

"I have no fucking idea, Jake. You think this is easy for me?"

"Jesus Christ!" he mutters.

"Not on the menu," I quip. "St. Pauli Girl's as holy as we get."

CHAPTER THIRTY-THREE

Kate

I don't know why I'm here, or for how long. But all I care about is Jake. I want him to find the love and happiness that eluded him with me. Sure, I'd like redemption—but only if, in my redemption, Jake can find salvation.

Jake's upset when he awakens the following morning. I sense that like a sonic boom. He wants desperately to believe that last night was nothing more than a bad dream. I'm dead. He knows that. I can plainly feel the question reverberating through his mind. *Am I crazy?*

"Okay, wait," he says out loud, to no one in particular. He'll address me now, he thinks, to prove last night was a once-in-a-lifetime delusion. Too much to drink, perhaps. "Kate!" he yells at the top of his lungs.

"I'm dead, not deaf!" I scream through his head. He jumps as if stunned by a cattle prod.

"Okay, okay, okay," he says, almost hyperventilating. "If this is really happening . . . if I'm not certifiable . . . then we need some ground rules. I can't have you in my head 24-7, Kate. I *will* go crazy then!"

"Fine. What ground rules would you suggest?"

"For starters, I don't want you accompanying me on dates!"

"Threesomes are hot, Jake!"

"Come on, Kate. I'm trying to be serious here."

"Okay," I say. I'm not sure if I mean it, but barring some emergency, it seems like a request I should honor. "What else."

"You don't get to decide what I want or need in life. *I* make those decisions."

"I only want what's best for you, Jake."

"I've got a mother for that," he snaps.

"Okay. But I get to make suggestions."

"I can't fucking believe this," he mutters, hands on his temples.

"What?"

"I'm negotiating with a fucking ghost!"

"Look, Jake, I only want to help."

"I can't see how this is helping."

"You will, I promise."

The onus is now on me. If I'm not going to be just a thorn in Jake's side, I'll need to adhere to a plan. It begins with baseball.

CHAPTER THIRTY-FOUR

Jake

The Scorpions are away this weekend, but I abandon my home-only commitment to travel with the team. I made that commitment to spend time at home with my live wife, not my dead wife. I could have spent the weekend with Lorna, but Kate foiled that.

Fats and Barney pencil me in for Saturday night in Waco. If I'm lucky, the range of Kate's telepathic travel is limited to Tucson. It doesn't take long to learn otherwise.

Waco's leadoff batter steps to the plate. My catcher is Roddy Baker, nicknamed "Closing Time," or "C.T.," for his penchant for being the last man out of the tavern. Roddy played three seasons of minor league ball for the Rangers. He's tough as a stump, baseball-savvy, and an unapologetic boozer. It's this last trait that ended his otherwise promising career.

I peer in for the sign. Roddy drops down a single finger, wiggling it away from the batter: fastball, outside. As I'm about to begin my motion, I hear that voice.

"He's looking 'dead red'; throw 'im a curve." *What the fuck?* I step off the rubber.

"What the fuck do you think you're doing," I mutter, under my breath, to Kate.

"What's so hard to understand?" she says. "I read his mind. He's looking fastball, so throw him a curve!"

I'm peeved, but return to the rubber and check for the sign. Unaware of Kate's intercession, C. T. again signals for the fastball, away. I shake him off. He changes the sign: two fingers—curveball. The batter lunges, missing the pitch by a foot.

We repeat the process. Again, I shake off the sign and throw what Kate orders. Strike two. The umpire rings up the batter on my third pitch, a changeup ordered by Kate in lieu of the curve the hitter's expecting. C. T. plods to the mound for a chat.

"What the goddamn fuck are you doing?" he asks me. I'm not sure how to respond. *I'm waiting for my dead wife to read the batter's mind and order up a pitch to fool him.* I can't say that.

"Tell him you're sorry," Kate suggests. "I'll speed up the process. You'll be fine."

"Sorry, C. T., something got in my eye." I rub it to buttress the subterfuge. "Still a little blurry, so how 'bout you slow down your signs a bit."

"Whatever the fuck you say, Ace," Roddy says, spitting onto the mound and strutting back to the plate.

With Kate's incredibly annoying but uncannily effective help, I mow down the first twelve batters. Barney, my pitching coach, sidles up to me in the dugout while we bat in the fifth.

"Who the heck are you talking to out there?"

"Whaddya mean?" I ask, innocently.

"You're babbling a mean streak between every pitch," Barney observes. "What's that about?"

"A new approach," I ad lib. "Sort of like visualization—you know, where the athlete visualizes what he wants to accomplish before he executes? Only in my case, I talk myself through it."

Barney shakes his head and smiles. "That's a crock of shit," he says. "But you can stand on your fucking head or do cartwheels, as far as I'm concerned, if you get results. So, keep it up, whatever the fuck it is, okay Einstein?"

"Sure, Barney."

Kate's been nothing if not efficient. Her reads come more quickly, but I shake off nearly half of C.T.'s signs, which is pissing him off. We cruise through the next four innings, nursing a 2-0 lead through eight. I've yet to allow a hit.

Ballplayers are notoriously superstitious, particularly in the course of no-hitters. No one sits within six feet of me on the bench. I'm quarantined, as if diagnosed with the plague. Truth is, I prefer it this way. I can listen to Kate without any distraction.

"I'm concerned," she says, "about the third guy up in the ninth. He's been harder to read each time up. Just a warning—I might have nothing on him this time."

"Hmmm," I mutter, hoping no one notices me conversing with my dead wife while on the verge of a no-hitter.

Kate works her magic on the first two batters in the ninth. As the third hitter strides to the plate, I await her advice.

"Getting nothing relevant, Jake. He's fantasizing about fucking the fat girl in the first row behind his dugout. I think he knows her."

I step off the rubber. "I'll handle this," I say. C. T. calls for a curve to start. I comply. Might be the best breaking ball I've thrown all night. Strike one. Closing Time flips the ball back, returns to his crouch, and signals fastball, down and away. Strike two.

I'm one strike away from a no-hitter. The crowd is buzzing. I exhale deeply, consulting C.T. for the sign. Change up, away, he orders.

"No!" Kate wails. "He's paying attention now, looking for

something off-speed. Give 'im a fastball, up." I back off the rubber, motioning Closing Time to the mound for a conference. It gives me time to think.

"What are you, some kind of spirit prodigy?" I ask Kate, while C. T. slogs to the mound. "Where'd you learn all this stuff?"

"Mostly from Nick. He's a genius."

She's learned from the best, so I feel even more confident with her call.

Closing Time reaches the mound. "What the fuck do you want now?"

"I wanna throw a fastball, up," I tell him.

"Don't think so, Ace. He's a high-ball hitter. Played with him in the Frontier League coupl'a years back."

"My mind's made up," I say.

"It's your no-hitter," he says, depositing another hefty gob of saliva at my feet as he returns to the plate.

"Isn't it bad luck for him to mention your no-hitter?" Kate asks, mentioning my no-hitter.

"I don't believe that shit," I say.

"No, but you believe in ghosts," she counters.

"Touché."

By now, the crowd is standing, anticipating the completion of my gem. C. T. squats behind the plate. He flashes the sign for the high fastball. I wind up and fire.

POW! The batter hammers it fifty feet over the centerfield fence.

"Fuckin' told you!" bellows Closing Time.

"Dammit!" I scream.

"Sorry, Jake," says Kate, earnestly. "I'll make it up to you." I've heard that one before.

CHAPTER THIRTY-FIVE

Jake

"FOUR-FINGER SINGER LOSES NO-HIT BID WITH TWO OUTS IN NINTH." So reads the headline on the sports page of the *Daily Star*. I haven't heard a peep from Kate since leaving the mound on Saturday night. Fats yanked me after the home run. "Fuckin' good game," he said, "goddamn fuckin' mammoth home run notwithstanding." A reliever secured the last out, preserving the victory.

"Wish I'd been there," Nick says, peeking into my office on Monday morning.

"Sit down," I say soberly.

"What's up?" He flashes me a look of concern. "You okay?"

"I spent all day yesterday debating whether to tell you this," I say. "But I'm gonna explode if I don't tell somebody."

Nick looks at me with alarm. "Tell me what?"

"You're gonna think I'm fucking crazy."

"You've got my attention."

"Kate speaks to me."

"Kate . . . your dead wife, Kate . . . speaks to you?"

"Right."

"You're fucking crazy."

"I knew you'd say that."

"How does she speak to you?"

"She gets into my head, but her voice is plain as day."

"Does anyone else hear it?"

"Well, no."

"Do you *see* her?"

"Yeah," I say, pointing at my office door. "She's standing right over there by the door." Nick swivels around in his chair.

"There's no—"

"I know, Nick. That was a cheap courtroom trick. Proves there's a small part of you that wants to believe me." I smile smugly. "But no, I don't see her."

"So, give me an example."

There's no way I'm going to chronicle Kate's interference with my attempted liaison with Lorna O'Malley. So, I explain what happened in Waco.

"You're telling me Kate helped you nearly pitch a no-hitter?"

"Well, until the last pitch, when she sort of wandered off-script. She's using pitch-calling skills she claims to have learned from you."

"From me?" That revelation gives him momentary pause. "Come on, Jake. Do you really expect me to believe this?"

"I don't know what to expect, Nick," I say, my angst renewed. "There's no way in hell any of this makes any sense to me. But it's happening. I swear."

"Okay, look. I wanna believe you, but what you're telling me strains credulity, to say the least. Maybe you should take a few days off."

"I don't *want* any time off. I can't just sit around the house . . . and do nothing."

"Fine. I've got a better idea. I'll make you an appointment with my sister-in-law's husband. You remember, the therapist. Let him help you sort out your emotions. It's been only a few weeks, Jake. And, you have to admit, your behavior has been somewhat... shall we say... *erratic*, beginning with the funeral. Let me make you that appointment. Please, Jake."

The more I think about it, the more inclined I am to accept Nick's offer. He's right on one count—my reaction to Kate's death was hardly conventional. And maybe I am imagining all this conversation with Kate. "You win," I say. "Make the appointment."

Later that day, I sit down with Christie. She's been working overtime to keep my clients on the rails while I muddle through, distracted by Kate's death, Lorna O'Malley, Kate's resurrection, and baseball, in roughly that sequence.

"I'm sorry I've left you holding the bag," I say, sitting in her small office just down the hall from my own. "I really appreciate what you've done."

"It's okay, Jake. Glad to help." She sounds chipper, but I can't help but think she's masking deeper emotions. So am I. I feel as if I've taken Christie for granted. She's been devoted to me, supportive during the odious Pastor Bastard affair. She's admitted her ardor for me and then, like the professional she is, faithfully observed the protocols of decorum. I feel guilty for succumbing to a fling with Lorna, a mere week after Kate's death, while distancing myself from Christie in compliance with the unwritten mandates applying to recent widowers and employers alike.

She spends the next half hour briefing me on everything I've neglected since the funeral, reminding me, in the process, how much I admire her.

CHAPTER THIRTY-SIX

Kate

"Jake!"

"What!" he screams, startled, spilling his coffee all over himself at the kitchen table. "Jesus, Kate, can't you ring a little bell or something to warn me you're here?"

"I'd need hands for that, Jake, wouldn't I?"

"Okay, point taken. *Why* are you here?"

"I live here?"

"You *lived* here, Kate. You're dead now, remember?"

"Yeah, Jake, that's the thing. You know that and I know that. So, what's this bullshit about seeing a shrink?"

"It was Nick's idea."

"Why would Nick suggest you see a shrink?"

"Because I told him about you."

"Why in God's name did you do *that*?" I'm more than a little displeased. I don't want my presence turning into a carnival. It's why I've limited my communications solely to Jake.

"Because I'm going nuts here, Kate. Exhibit One: I talk to my dead wife!"

"And how's a shrink gonna change that?"

"Well, maybe I *am* crazy. Maybe you're just a figment of my imagination."

"Do you really believe that? Didn't we just nearly pitch a no-hitter together, Einstein? Wasn't I there for you, every step of the way?"

"Well, there was that pitch you called in the ninth," he chuckles, "you know, the one that was pummeled to kingdom come?"

"I'm still perfecting my craft, Jake. Anyway, what do I have to do to prove to you that I exist?"

"Nothing, Kate. Look, don't take it personally. You've got to admit this is weird. Let's say I'm seeing the shrink to appease Nick. Let's go with that, okay?"

"Sure, Jake, whatever you say."

An attractive, well-dressed blonde in her thirties exits Dr. Robert Weaver's office while Jake thumbs through magazines in the psychologist's waiting room. Moments later, the shrink himself walks up to Jake, thrusting out his hand and introducing himself. Jake returns the handshake and follows him into his office. The doc sits on one of a pair of wing chairs in the front of the office; Jake claims the other. A leather couch occupies the space opposite them; behind the couch is the doctor's desk.

"Nick is very fond of you," Dr. Weaver says. "Says the two of you went to Stanford together." And blah, blah, blah.

I almost missed the appointment—not that I'd been invited. Once again, I wound up in a parking lot on the first try, before honing in on the doctor's couch. I've yet to announce my presence to Jake, figuring he might be less than appreciative. I just want to make sure this quack doesn't undo all of what I've been working to accomplish.

"Tell me about your relationship with Kate—uh, before her untimely passing," the doc says to Jake once he's satisfied himself that, but for his tendency to converse with his dead wife, he isn't otherwise looney-tunes.

He gets an earful out of that question. Jake tells him

everything—about what he calls my "obsession" with baby-making, about how Pastor Bastard—uh, Pastor Becker—and Billy Garabedian took "repeated advantage" of what Jake calls my "gullibility." I have to admit, the picture he paints is hardly a recipe for marital longevity. But, as Jake takes pains to repeat on several occasions, he loved me, despite it all. He doesn't just say that for my benefit, I hasten to point out, because he doesn't yet know I'm here. Anyway, he reveals that he'd not yet decided whether our marriage was "salvageable" when I managed my unscheduled rendezvous with that idiot trucker. Maybe I should have evaded that big rig after all.

"And how did you feel when you learned of the accident?" the doctor asks him. "After the initial sense of shock, that is."

"Sadness, anger, guilt, confusion," he says, along with a couple of twenty-five cent words I've never even heard before.

"And how would you characterize your encounters with Kate now . . . that is, *since* her death?" the shrink inquires, as if such circumstances weren't the least bit out of the ordinary.

"Intrusive, annoying—"

"What the fuck, Jake!" I scream into his head. I can't help myself. He flinches, then scowls, surveying the room, as if he expects to actually see me.

"Speak of the devil," Jake deadpans, "the guest of honor has arrived." With that revelation, even Doc Weaver scans the room.

"Where? Do you see her anywhere in this office?" he asks, trying not to sound too patronizing.

"No, Doc. I told you. It's only in my head."

"And what did she just say?"

"She said, and I quote, 'what the fuck, Jake!'"

"'What the fuck, Jake?'" he repeats.

"Yeah, Doc, 'what the fuck, Jake,'" I interject.

"There! She said it again," Jake informs him.

"She said 'what the fuck, Jake' again?" Doc asks.

"Yes. Right. 'What the fuck.'" Jake replies.

This is getting tedious, I think. So, apparently, does Dr. Weaver. I remain silent for a while, to atone for my outburst.

"Tell me, Jake," the doctor says, "how Kate first made her presence known to you."

"It's actually a little embarrassing," he says. Dr. Weaver nods, pinching his lips, urging Jake to continue. "I was having sex with my next-door neighbor," he begins.

"Your . . . next-door neighbor?" Dr. Weaver repeats. Why do shrinks repeat everything?

"Uh, yeah. Long story, but the point is that she yelled 'Stop! Fucking stop!' just as we were about to make love."

"Let me be sure I've got this straight. Kate yelled 'Stop . . . fucking stop' when you were about to make love to your neighbor?"

"That's right."

"What happened then?"

"I thought it was my neighbor asking me to stop, so I stopped."

"And then?"

"She said she hadn't said anything."

"Your neighbor?"

"Right. So, as I was about to . . . uh . . . resume, Kate made some crack about Lorna's pubic hair."

"Lorna's your neighbor?"

"Right. That her pubic hair wasn't red."

"That her pubic hair wasn't red?" *Jesus, would you shut the fuck up and let Jake talk?*

"She's a redhead, you see—"

"Kate?"

"No, Lorna."

"Oh, for God's sake, Jake," I blurt out. "You're wasting your time with this dickwad!"

"You're right," Jake says, out loud.

"About what?" Dr. Dickwad asks.

"Sorry, doc, I guess I was responding to my wife's latest comment."

"Which was?"

"'For God's sake, Jake. You're wasting your time with this dickwad.' Sorry, doc, but that's an exact quote."

"Look, Jake, I don't think you're taking this very seriously," Dr. Dickwad opines.

"Actually, Dr. Weaver, I'm not sure *you're* taking this seriously," Jake responds. *You tell 'im, Jake!*

"Look, Jake. This is all pretty textbook. You were acting out on your frustrations and tangled emotions by having an ill-timed affair with your neighbor." I've got to agree with Dr. Dickwad on that score. "You were having second thoughts about what you were about to pursue with this . . . uh . . . Lorna, when you imagined your wife's interrupting the act. It allowed you to relieve yourself of guilt or shame by shifting the blame onto an imaginary figure—in this case, Kate."

Jake just sits there, staring into space. Weaver's theory is bullshit, he thinks. Of course, I *know* it's bullshit—and I've had quite enough of his arrogant drivel, thank you.

"Jake," I say to him. "Tell Doc Weaver that he's full of shit. Then tell him that I know that he's spent more of this hour thinking about how he just fucked Hilda, the blonde who just left this office, than listening to you."

Jake grins conspiratorially. The shrink notices, deducing at once that Jake has been privy to yet another imagined revelation from his dead wife. "What did she just tell you this time?" he asks wearily.

"I don't think you want to know."

"Tell me, Jake. It's your inner self gradually breaking through the barriers you've erected to sustain you in your grief."

"She said that you've been fantasizing much of this session about how you just, to paraphrase my *imaginary* spouse, concluded an adulterous liaison with that blond woman who left your office before our session began." Weaver's jaw slackens. "Her name is . . . what was it, Kate?"

"Hilda," I say.

"Hilda," Jake repeats. Dr. Weaver drops his notepad and turns purple.

"O—okay," he stutters. "I sense some aggression now. Let's explore—"

"Jake," I say. "Mention the black bra she left to amuse him. He's been thinking about it since he discovered she'd left it right there on his desk chair."

Jake smiles. If he has any lingering doubts as to my existence, they're now long gone. He gets up slowly, looking the shrink in the eye. He walks toward the desk. "Kate says Hilda left a black bra on your desk chair."

Dr. Weaver shoots up like a piston, blocking Jake's advance around his desk. "Okay, okay!" he says, breathlessly. "I don't know how the hell you could have known that, but it's freaking me out. I . . . I'm not going to charge you for this session. I don't think I can do anything for you. And," he adds, his cheeks still flushed, "I'd appreciate your discretion in this other matter, which is really none of your concern."

"Well played, Kate," Jake says, laughing his way out the door.

CHAPTER THIRTY-SEVEN

Jake

I've come to terms with the lingering existence of my dead wife. It's taken time to get used to the idea, particularly her unannounced visits, but I find her companionship both agreeable and amusing—most of the time. On the other hand, with no idea how long this is likely to continue, I fear she'll become like the houseguest who overstays her welcome.

"How'd it go with Doc Weaver?" Nick asks on the morning after my visit to the shrink.

"He's cheating on your wife's sister," I say.

Nick blanches. "What?"

"Kate figured it out. Quite a coup, I thought." Look, I have more allegiance to Nick, and by extension, his family, than to Dr. Dickwad.

Nick takes a seat in my office and invites me to elaborate. He doesn't know what to believe anymore. He *prefers* to believe that I'm bonkers. It'll take his sister-in-law's husband off the hook, and relieve him from the quandary of what, if anything, to say to his wife.

"Look, Nick. I know you think I'm nuts, and I'm okay with that. But I thought I owed it to you to tell you."

"Okay, Jake. Thanks." He gets up, shakes his head, and leaves my office. I think he's still inclined to believe I'm batshit crazy.

Crazy or not, my collaboration with Kate on the ball field continues, with increasingly impressive results. By early June, we'd won all five of our starts. The sportswriters cover my outings with the zeal generally reserved for University of Arizona football and basketball, which is to say that I'm front-page news. I've been interviewed several times, neglecting on each occasion to assign proper credit to my dead wife. Sure, I say she's been "an inspiration," but I can hardly describe her mind-reading contributions now, can I?

My next outing changes everything. It's a road contest against the Amarillo Armadillos. I'm well on my way to another shutout when, returning to the dugout after pitching the sixth, I see a familiar face in the stands behind home plate. Clutching a radar gun in his right hand, he flashes me a smile. It's that hoary old scout—and my father's nemesis—Harley McGinniss of the Cleveland Indians.

Kate and I win the game handily. Harley awaits me, pulling me aside as I emerge from the clubhouse. "Can we talk, Jake?"

I'm delighted to see him. As rotund as ever, he harbors a chaw of tobacco in his swollen left cheek. We arrange to meet an hour later at a bar near our no-star hotel.

Harley's generous frame engulfs a barstool near the front door of Shorty's Bar & Grill. "Let's grab a table," he says, intercepting me as I enter. Shorty's is big with the cowboy demographic. We feel naked without our cowboy boots and ten-gallon hats. Harley grabs his whiskey, as well as a glass he's reserved for me, and moves to a table in the back of the bar.

"So, what brings you to Amarillo, of all places?" I ask.

"You, of course."

"Me?"

"That's right." He downs his whiskey in a single gulp.

"Sorry, I'm not sure what you mean."

"Come on, Jake. I'm a *scout*. Word is you're thirty-three going on twenty-one. Throwing like the hot-shot young buck you were, back in the day."

"It's the Tex-Ar-Mex League, Harley. Can't get much lower."

"Granted, it's not Triple-A," he concedes. "But you're mowing 'em down like it's Little League, and these guys are better than that. Your stuff is as good as it ever was; your breaking pitch is way better and your control's off the charts. God knows why you waited over a decade to get back into the saddle."

"Some fucker chopped off my finger, Harley. Reoriented my thinking." I take a swig of my whiskey.

"Regrettable, of course. But not fatal." He winces. "Geez, I shouldn'ta said that . . . with your wife and all. Really sorry 'bout your wife, Jake."

"Thanks, Harley. It's okay. And look, I appreciate your acknowledgment of my improvement, but what's your point?"

"I wanna sign you, Jake. I know it's a flyer, but the Indians are right in the thick of the pennant race, and with the injuries we've had, we're thin on the mound. We're working all angles, and this is a promising one."

"Come on, Harley. I'm way too old to start all over again, you know that."

"I want you to start at Double-A, Akron, in the Eastern League. Make a few appearances, see what happens. If you click, we'll promote you to Triple A Columbus and then . . . well, next step's The Show."

I drain my drink unconsciously. "Look, Harley, I really appreciate your interest, but I'm an adult. I've got a job. A life." Even as I say it, I realize how little those things mean to me, now that the flesh-and-bones Kate is gone.

"All I'm asking is that you think about it. Mull it over a few days." He smiles and leans toward me. "You've been waiting for this opportunity your whole life. What've you got to lose?"

"You're doing this, Jake!" Kate says, excitedly, seconds after I return to my tawdry hotel room. "No ifs, ands, or buts!" I'm hardly surprised to learn she'd been eavesdropping at the bar.

"Getting around pretty well now, aren't you, Kate. No more parking lot misadventures?"

"Old hat now."

"Upgraded the app on your spectral GPS?"

She ignores my little joke. "So?"

"So, what?"

"Come on, asshole. Gonna sign or what?"

"Like I told Harley, I'm an adult. Can't just chuck all my responsibilities for an all-expense-paid trip to Akron."

"What responsibilities? Don't have to support your dead wife. No kids. You're footloose and fancy free."

"My clients might not see it that way."

"You've been neglecting them for weeks. Your girlfriend's handling things quite well, I gather."

"Colleague, Kate. Not girlfriend. We're not going to beat that dead—" Not all idioms are appropriate for discussions with the deceased. "Sorry, no offense."

"None taken," she says. "You've dreamed of this chance for most of your life. I'm not about to let you pass it up."

I sit down on the bed. "Look, Kate. I'll admit this has been fun. But it's as ephemeral as you are. None of it is real."

"What's *ephemeral* mean, Einstein?"

"Fleeting, short-lived. And what happens when . . . or if . . . you're not out there reading batters' minds for me? What am I then?"

"Is that what you're afraid of? That's not me throwing that 'stuff' that Harley likes so much with the 'off-the-charts control' he says you've got. You could kick ass without my help."

She lets that sink in, awaiting my reaction. I don't want to give her the impression she's making headway, but she is. And then she offers up a challenge: "Tell you what, Jake. You do it on your own next week. If you fall flat on your face, you go back to your little cubbyhole and crank out reams of *heretos* and *whereases*. But if you pitch like I know you'll pitch, you sign that goddamn contract and give it a whirl. What's the worst that can happen? You fail? Hey, that's nothing like getting splattered by an eighteen-wheeler now, is it?"

CHAPTER THIRTY-EIGHT

Jake

It's mind-boggling, really, that my wife is so much wiser in death than she was in life. There's now a clever and perspicacious metaphorical head on those non-existent shoulders. Kate still knows how to press my buttons, to be sure, but she does so to surprisingly good effect.

I take her up on her challenge to 'go it alone.' Unaccompanied by the Late, Great Kate, I stand astride the mound at Tucson Electric Park on the following Saturday night. This is the precipice to which she has cleverly maneuvered me. I'll have no more excuses. Without a mind-reading, pitch-calling phantom to rely on, I may fall flat on my face. I'll know, then, that anything more than a sideline as a weekend hurler in a two-bit semi-pro league is a figment of my imagination—like Kate herself, perhaps. I can then embrace my life at Davis, Davis & Singer, reburying my long-abandoned dreams of The Show, and, quite possibly, my late wife, too. If, on the other hand, I 'kick ass' without help from my nearly departed, I'll know that I'm capable of one last shot at The Show.

Finishing my warm-ups, I gaze into the stands. There, in the third row behind the dugout again, is the voluptuous Lorna O'Malley. She's impossible to overlook, her red hair a beacon in the withering sunlight. Whether she's smiling at me or just thrilled to have jettisoned her kids for the weekend, I can't be sure, but she's here just the same. Behind home plate sit Nick and Christie. With Trudy spending the evening consoling her sister—who'd banished her cheating psychologist husband from the house—Nick offered her ticket to Christie. She's not yet seen me pitch, probably afraid that taking the initiative to do so was somehow inappropriate, but less so when the ticket comes from the partner in charge of office decorum.

In the first row behind home plate sits Harley McGinniss, a radar gun in his left hand and a Styrofoam cup in his right—a makeshift receptacle for the tobacco-laced sputum that will bleed from his mouth over the course of the evening. And I know that somewhere in this vast ballpark, in the blistering desert heat, lurks the indomitable spirit of the late Kate Singer.

I've already soaked through my uniform when the leadoff batter steps to the plate for the Corpus Christi Caballeros.

"Ball, outside!" roars the umpire, in heroic understatement, as my first pitch sails to the backstop. C.T. retrieves the errant baseball, utters a choice expletive, and fires it back with authority. I glare at him, promenade around the mound, and return to the rubber.

Roddy calls for a fastball, low and away. I rear back, and fire it well into the next county. "Time!" he yells at the umpire, wrenching off his mask and stomping toward the mound. "What the *fuck* are you doing, Einstein?" he implores me. I'm not sure, really. Accustomed to having my head filled with advice and information from Kate, I find it hard to adjust to the silence between my temples.

"Gimme a break, C.T.," I plead. "It's only two-and-oh."

"Fuck," he belches, retreating in disgust.

I glance again into the stands, feeling woefully adrift. I think about Kate, Christie, Nick, and Lorna, dismayed at the clusterfuck my life has become. I converse with the dead and neglect my day job, neither of which endears me to my best friend. I wonder if Nick's shared with Christie his misgivings about my sanity. Does she adore me, despise me, or pity me?

Mired between self-loathing and self-doubt, I uncork a calamitous curveball that bounces fifteen feet in front of the plate before clanging off the batter's left knee. His shrieks reverberate through the ballpark as he slumps to the ground.

Closing Time whips off his mask and charges the mound, hurling at me a thesaurus of expletives. At the same time, Barney O'Toole launches himself from the dugout, advancing toward the mound like a serial killer on a mission.

"What the hell's wrong with you, Singer?" Barney hollers, words barely audible through the cascade of epithets and spittle spewing from the angry lips of my catcher. Before I can answer, another voice joins the chorus.

"You're making me sick out here, Jake!" It's the unmistakable voice of Kate. "If I could still vomit, I'd have done so by now!" she complains. "Pitch with your balls, Einstein, not your head! Stop being a chickenshit and *get it together, for God's sake*!"

"I'm fine," I shout at Barney and C.T., waving them off like gnats. "Just leave me the fuck alone!" They stalk off, leaving trails of profanity and saliva in their wakes.

"Thanks, Kate," I mutter, as I climb back onto the rubber. Her rebuke has liberated me from the fog of my ill-timed malaise.

I'm as focused as a laser as the next batter steps to the plate. As suddenly as it abandoned me, it all comes rushing back: my 93-mile-per-hour heater, that devastating curve, the confounding change-up, and my pinpoint control. The rest of the night is all mine. It reminds me of my days of Little League domination. Fourteen punch-outs and nary a walk. A couple of seeing-eye singles and a fly ball misplayed into a double—that's all Corpus Christi can muster.

Harley meets me in the clubhouse after the game, a self-satisfied grin on his face. "Here," he says, shoving a sheaf of papers at my chest. "Ten-grand signing bonus, relocation allowance. You report to Akron in a week."

"I'll think about it, Harley," I say.

"Don't overthink it, Jake. Here's my number. Call me in a couple of days." He gives me his card and a fatherly pat on the rump. "You'll never forgive yourself if you don't at least try."

Nick and Christie are gone when I emerge from the clubhouse. It's just as well—I don't know what to say to them. Lorna, however, is still here, waiting for me behind the dugout. I can no longer ignore her.

"I know a nice bar not far from here," she says. "Let me buy you a drink."

I've avoided Lorna for weeks now—since Kate engineered our embarrassing *coitus interruptus*. Though still uncertain whether to pursue a relationship with this woman, I'm cowed by her beauty and the plaintive look in those sparkling green eyes.

"Not a word!" I snap at Kate, wherever she may be, after I accept Lorna's offer.

CHAPTER THIRTY-NINE

Kate

You don't know boring until you've been dead. They don't call it 'dead time' for nothing. It's ten in the morning and they're still in the bedroom, squeals of pleasure emanating from Big Red for the third time since they hit the sheets last night. And I'm here in the living room, respecting the promise Jake extracted from me, not to interfere with his 'dates.' But this is no date—it's more like a carnival ride.

Think about it. It's not like I can grab the remote and watch Seinfeld reruns all night. Or flip through a pile of magazines. Instead, I hover around the neighborhood while I wait for the rodeo to end. When she finally leaves after brunch, I'm all over him.

"Jesus, Jake, she grunts like a javelina!"

"God dammit, Kate, you promised not to—"

"I wasn't there, Jake. I was here, in the living room, until you got up. Then flitted around the neighborhood till she left." He groaned.

"How am I going to keep you out of my love life?"

"Take me to court. Get a restraining order. Your honor," I mimic, "my dead wife is becoming a nuisance. I'd like an order keeping her out of my house when I'm fucking my neighbor!" Jake smiles. He's clearly getting used to me.

"Okay, Kate. Why are you here?" he asks. He's in the kitchen, clearing away the brunch dishes. "Am I due for another pep talk?"

"Depends," I say. "Are you gonna sign that contract?"

Jake shakes his head while meticulously loading the dishwasher. He always lines up the dishes like toy soldiers in perfect formation. Everything he does requires care and forethought. My spontaneity alternately pleased and unnerved him. "Haven't decided yet," he mutters.

"Life here's just too good? You think Lorna's gonna be content fucking you every weekend? You don't think she's looking for a sugar daddy for those four kids? Somehow, I don't see you in that role, Jake. No offense."

"None taken." He shuts the dishwasher and slinks into the living room, plunging into his favorite armchair. "Look, Kate. I wanna do it . . . I really do." He rubs his temples, trying to shake off the weariness wrought by a night of drinking and wanton sex. "But walking away from responsibilities is not who I am."

Jake can be so exasperating! "Your primary responsibility is to yourself," I blather, "to your happiness. Nick and Christie can deal with your clients; if they need more help, they can hire it. That's how businesses work."

"Nick made a commitment to me when he hired me. His Dad retired, knowing I'd assume his practice. Nick counted on that."

"And what if you hadn't taken the job? Someone else would have. Right?"

Jake gets up and opens the blinds. By now, the summer sun has risen above the roofline, eliminating the need for shade. He's obviously torn.

"Ask them for a leave of absence," I suggest, "through the end of the baseball season. It's already the end of July. That's just two or three months . . . months that could change your life forever."

"I'll discuss it with Nick tomorrow," he says. I can tell he's still wavering. The meeting with Nick could go either way. I definitely need to be present.

Jake sticks his head into Nick's office. "Got a minute?"

Five minutes later we're both in Nick's office. Jake reveals his offer from Harley. He doesn't immediately insist on a leave of absence, as I hoped he would. Instead, he presents the facts like a goddamn lawyer, hoping that Nick will make the decision for him. It doesn't go as he planned.

"Look, Jake," Nick says. "I know it's been a tough few months for you. And I know I was the one who urged you to play ball again. But you're not a little kid anymore. You can't just run away and join the circus."

"I was thinking about a leave of absence—just until the season's over." *That's better, Jake.*

"And what about your clients? Christie's working nights and weekends as it is." There's frustration in Nick's voice.

I can't keep quiet any longer. "He thinks you're a nutcase, Jake. Thinks guilting you out and tying you to your desk is gonna make me go away and restore your sanity. Fuck that, Jake! Be your own man! Tell him you're doing it, and if he doesn't like it, he can find someone to take your place!" Jake grimaces as I scold him, then emits a deep sigh.

"You okay?" Nick asks.

"No, Nick, I'm not." *Go Jake!* "My life is a fucking mess. I've got no wife and no life, but I've still got my dream . . . a shot at The Show. What have I got to lose? Will there ever be a better time to take a chance?" Jake vaults out of his chair. "I'm signing the contract, Nick. I'm sorry for the burden it'll cause, but I've got to do this. Call it a leave or replace me. It's up to you. I'll work out my transition with Christie. I'm leaving on Friday."

Nick shakes his head in resignation. "You gotta do what you gotta do," he shrugs. "Good luck, buddy." He extends his hand to Jake and manages a halfhearted smile.

As hard as the meeting had been with Nick, it's even tougher with Christie. When he tells her he's leaving, she begins to tear up. Jake may have noticed the moistened eyes, but I'm privy to her thoughts. She's devastated. There isn't a bit of doubt in my mind anymore: she absolutely adores him. As best I can tell, Nick hasn't yet burdened Christie with his concerns about Jake's mental health. So far as she knows, I'm emphatically dead.

"I'll miss you, Jake," she says, maintaining a brave front, "but I know how much this means to you. I'm rooting for you. Big time."

"I saw you in the crowd with Nick the other night," Jake says. "Glad you came."

"You were wonderful," she gushes, "despite that shaky start."

"Mind was playing games with me, but we—uh, I—got over it."

They're both silent for several moments.

"Look, Jake. I can handle the workload. You've been a great mentor. Nick can help me with anything that gets tricky until you come back. It's only a few months. I'll survive."

Jake is melting. I can feel it. Though he won't admit it to me, I know how much he cares for her. But there's something surreal about this conversation. It isn't what's being said. It's what *isn't* being said. Here sit two beautiful people, burdened with lawyers' personalities—cautious to a fault, conscious of the rules of the workplace, not to mention the social conventions that apply to everyone—everyone, that is, but Big Red.

Something about this fucked-up situation demands my attention, don't you think?

CHAPTER FORTY

Jake

Akron, Ohio. The Trenton of the Rust Belt. Used to be the Rubber Capital of the World—tires, not condoms—until European tire makers kicked our derrières. But, like Kate, the city that seemingly died is back from the grave.

Nowhere is this more apparent than at Canal Park, the sleek downtown stadium that's home to the Akron Aeros, the Double-A farm club of the Cleveland Indians. Here I stand, on Friday afternoon, August 9, 2013, the newest Aero, eager as a teenager, a suitcase in one hand and a gym bag in the other, three hours before game time.

After persuading a wary security guard to admit me to the park, I find my way to the clubhouse. Directed to the manager's office, I rap on the door. A gruff voice beckons me inside.

"Hey, Skip," I say. "I'm Jake Singer."

"So?" replies Fast Eddie Fernandez, a career minor leaguer who, a quarter century earlier, squeezed out a couple of dozen at bats at The Show. He's small and wiry, maybe fifty or so. Fast Eddie tips back in his office chair, his stocking feet perched on his desk. "Who the fuck let you in?"

"I'm your new left-hander," I announce, figuring he hadn't yet gotten the word.

He looks me over skeptically. "Right. And I'm Abraham Fucking Lincoln."

I put down my gym bag and suitcase. "Look, Skip. I just flew in from Tucson. I know you've got a game tonight and I'm good to go. I'm fresh. Last pitched almost a week ago."

"How old are you?"

"Thirty-three."

"Thirty-fucking-three?" And then he notices my left hand. "You did say left-hander, right?" Fast Eddie suddenly lets out a massive guffaw, springs from his chair, and pokes his head out the door. "Jackson!" he bellows, "get the fuck in here!" He returns to his chair, muttering. "Thirty-three-year-old left-hander with four fingers! Good one!"

Jimmy Jackson, the Aeros pitching coach, is a former big leaguer who's doubled in girth since his long-ago playing days. "What is it, Eddie?"

"Almost had me going, there, Jackson."

"What're you talking about, Skip?"

"Four-fingered lefty? Who put you up to this?"

"Jeez, sorry, Skip. Forgot to tell you. You were out when the front office called." Jackson turns to me apologetically. "Sorry. You're Singer?"

"Yup."

"Wait a minute," Fernandez says. "You're for real? From Tucson? Indians ain't got no farm club in Tucson. Where'd you say you pitched last?"

"Tucson Scorpions in the Tex-Ar-Mex League."

"What the fuck league is that?"

"Just signed by Harley McGinniss," I explain.

"Since when is McGinniss scouting retirement communities?"

"All joking aside," I say, "I'm here to pitch."

"Front office says he pitched in the Red Sox organization . . . like a decade ago," Jackson explains, "before somebody chopped off his finger. That right, Singer?"

"That about covers it," I acknowledge.

Fast Eddie shakes his head one last time. "Okay, Singer. Can't always figure out what the fuck they're up to back in Cleveland, but you're here. Let's make the best of it. Jackson," he says, turning to his pitching coach, "get the clubhouse boy to give him a locker and uniform." He turns again to me. "We'll put you in the pen tonight. See, maybe, what grandpa's got left in that ancient left arm . . . and that funky, fucked-up hand." He's laughing as I leave his office, closing the door behind me.

My new teammates are as confounded by my age and deformity as my manager. At least there's something to talk about. Most of the players are at least a decade younger. I feel like a chaperone at a high school dance.

By the top of the ninth inning, the Aeros are trailing the Richmond Flying Squirrels (you read that right) by five runs. It's garbage time, the perfect opportunity to unveil McGinniss's Folly. As I stride in from the bullpen to start the inning, I feel that rush of adrenaline I recall from my days in Lowell and Trenton, seemingly a lifetime ago. Climbing up the mound to begin my warm-ups, a familiar voice pierces the ether.

"Hey, Jake," she says. "I'm here to help."

Kate's been absent since my meeting with Nick on Monday morning. I wondered if she'd finished with me, if her spectral errand had ended with my return to pro ball. I shudder to admit it, but I've missed her. Her company mitigates the loneliness of widowhood. And while Kate left me on my own—to prove a point—during my final outing with the Scorpions, we'd made a pretty good team before then. It was a treat to share my success with her—after all, pitching's not typically a conjugal activity.

"Thought maybe you'd found some other over-the-hill hurler to haunt," I whisper.

"Wouldn't dream of it, lover," she says.

"Okay, Kate," I mutter. "What's the batter anticipating?"

"Fastball. Dead red," she answers. Somehow, I picture her smiling broadly, just like I am.

I shake off the catcher's fastball sign, nodding when he calls for a curve. "Stee-. . . rike one!" the umpire bellows. Eight pitches later and we've struck out the side.

"Who the fuck *are* you?" howls Fernandez, as I return to the dugout, an impish smile plastered across my face.

CHAPTER FORTY-ONE

Jake

I spend all of a week in Akron. Three appearances, five scoreless innings. Harley attends that third game, his gelatinous rump ensconced in the stands behind home plate, his radar gun pointed at me like a six-shooter in a John Wayne western. Clad in his trademark plaid shirt, suspenders, and size 48 pants, he pulls me aside in the clubhouse after the game, waves me into Fast Eddie's empty office, and shuts the door.

"Bumping you up to Columbus," he says. The Columbus Clippers are the Indians' Triple-A franchise, the highest rung in the minor league ladder, a hair's breadth from The Show. "The big club's snakebit with injuries," he says, maneuvering his tongue around the wad in his cheek. "Down two starters in the last week." He picks up an empty coffee cup from the manager's desk, raises it to his mouth, and spits, twice. "Front office wants to stretch you out as a starter, Jake. Think you can handle that?"

My heart skips a beat. Grooming me to start when the major league rotation is riddled with injuries is like offering a termite a pile of wood chips to feast on. I try my best to sound nonchalant.

"Sure, Harley. No problem."

"Arm feels okay?"

"Never better."

"Okay, then. Pack your bags. You meet the club on the road in Durham tomorrow." He reaches into his pants pocket and pulls out a plane ticket. "Here. You'll need this. Good luck, kid."

"Jesus, Jake, why didn't you tell me?" Kate's whining punctures the stillness of the morning in my Durham hotel room.

"Tell you what, Kate?"

"That you'd been kicked upstairs to the Clippers. In Durham, North Carolina!"

"Never gave me your cellphone number," I quip. "And you *never* check your email anymore. Do I reach you through the Cloud? Or the dead letter office?"

"You're fucking hilarious, Jake," she says. "Think it's easy navigating in my condition? Takes a shitload of concentration. I've been all over Akron, parts of which can scare the crap out of a ghost. Finally overheard that skinny little runt of a manager tell someone you'd been shipped here." I figure she's done venting, but I'm wrong. "And do you have any idea how many hotels there are in Durham?"

"Lemme check TripAdvisor." I take out my cellphone, tap in the commands, and provide the answer: "Seventy." I can picture her fuming during the brief silence between her question and my answer.

"Okay, Jake. Fine. You've had your chuckle. So now I'm here."

"Right. You can now add Durham to your list of haunts."

"Enough banter. When do you pitch?"

"I start tomorrow night. Why?"

"Because we've got work to do."

I discover several things later that day. First, Kate has entered a new phase. Not content to simply read batters' minds, she's added pre-game planning to her repertoire. Somehow, she's gained access to the Durham Bulls' scouting reports on their own players. She's studied their tendencies, their individual strengths and weaknesses. It's what Nick and I used to do at Stanford, except we weren't privy to the opposition's internal work product.

"Isn't that a bit beyond the pale?" I ask her.

"Shit was left out in the open, just begging for me to take a peek! I can't open file drawers, you know."

"But—"

"Is it fair to try to steal signs?"

"Well," I say hesitantly, "that's fair game, I guess."

"Is it fair to read minds?"

"Harder question."

"You do your best using the resources at your disposal, right?"

"Yeah, Kate, but not everyone's got a mind-reading, blabber-mouthed dead wife to rely on, you know?"

"Their loss, not yours," she says. A lot of irony in those words, it seems to me, so I decide to end the inquiry there.

Kate sits me down and downloads the skinny she's compiled on each of the Bulls' hitters. I grab a pad and pencil from the hotel room desk.

She reels off players' names, tendencies against left-handed pitchers, power ratings. She tells me which are the dead-pull hitters, who pounds fastballs, what guys can't hit breaking pitches. "How the heck can you remember all that?" I ask her.

"No longer equipped to take notes," she boasts, "so I'm using my virtual mind. Gotta tell ya, Jake, it's a heckuva lot better than when I only had a brain." Kate was refining her skills on an almost daily basis. "You are going to The Show, Jake Singer, if I have to kill myself to get you there!"

CHAPTER FORTY-TWO

Kate

I'm hovering over the pitcher's mound at the *new* Durham *Bulls* Athletic Park, the one that replaced the *old* Durham Athletic Park, which is the one from the movie *Bull Durham.* I almost didn't get here. What kind of idiocy is it to give nearly identical names to two different ballparks in the same city? An hour ago, I was all alone in *Durham Athletic Park*, a dilapidated old stadium from the Ice Age, wondering where the hell everyone was! Half expected to see Kevin Costner flirting with Susan Sarandon behind the empty dugout.

Jake's on the mound when I finally arrive at the right ballpark.

"Where the hell were you?" he asks. I have to admit, I'm flattered by his concern.

"Durham Athletic Park," I say.

"This is Durham *Bulls* Athletic Park," he counters, as if the distinction is obvious.

"Could've used that advice an hour ago, Einstein."

"Never mind," he says, pounding the ball into his glove. "Let's get to work."

By now, our collaboration is virtually seamless. Sure, there are a few blips now and again, but nothing we can't work through. If he needs a moment to clarify or question me, he can step off the rubber and start again. I like that about baseball: there's no clock to force you into hasty mistakes.

That Jake babbles on the mound is now common knowledge. Not that he speaks to *me*. Everyone figures he just blabs to himself. The fans love that kind of quirkiness. Jake says there used to be a guy in the Seventies, a Tigers' pitcher named Mark "The Bird" Fidrych, who talked to himself on the mound when he pitched. But unless you're good, no one cares about your antics. And tonight, Jake is *way* beyond good.

I haven't left much to chance. From those scouting reports, I know the Bulls' shortstop can't handle a curve, so Jake feeds him a steady diet of breaking balls. Their big right fielder has a long swing, so Jake pounds him high and tight with fastballs he can't get around on. The first baseman keys on the fastball, so we give him everything but.

It's not just the intelligence I furnish him. Jake's stuff is unbelievable. His fastball is humming. His curve drops like an anchor. His slider breaks about three feet, bearing in on the righties and leaving lefties lunging. And just to keep the poor bastards on their toes, his changeup has batters flailing long before it arrives.

The big lug gets sharper as the game rolls on. By the start of the eighth inning, he's chalked up fourteen strikeouts while scattering four measly hits. But the Clippers' offense is equally feeble. So here we stand (or at least *he* does), in the last of the eighth inning of a scoreless contest.

Death's funny. A few months ago, I didn't know squat about baseball. Well, maybe I'd absorbed *something* being married to Jake, for as long as that lasted, and Nick had given me a crash course in the finer points at the first (and only) Scorpions' game I attended in the flesh. But the thing is, I'm way smarter now that I'm dead. My powers of concentration are phenomenal. I don't waste energy on physical concerns, and I've got no distractions. I focus like a laser, in a way that I never could in life. Not only that, but hanging around Jake, I've picked up the lingo, absorbing his baseball smarts like a sponge. Anyway, that's been my experience, and, unless you've discussed the matter with some other dead folks lately, you'll have to take my word for it.

Jake starts off the leadoff hitter with a pair of strikes, then wastes a fastball outside. I understand exactly what he's doing—he's setting up the chump for that devastating changeup of his.

"He's looking for a hard one," I advise my darling widower.

"'Course he is," Jake says, "so we'll pull the string." He coils into that big windup of his, rears back, and fires what, from his arm action, looks like another hard one. The overmatched batter swings at the motion, long before the ball plops harmlessly into the catcher's mitt for the third strike.

Next poor sucker has a notion to lay down a bunt. Easy, peasy. Jake throws it up in the strike zone. Guy pops it up, right into the waiting glove of our hero!

The third hitter plans on icing the game with one swing. Has the size to do it. We've thrown him high fastballs all night—well, Jake has. Catcher calls for a curve, down and away. Why not, I think. Galoot misses it by a mile. "Let's do it again," I say. "He's thinking fastball, hoping you'll throw it right into his sweet spot." Strike two. "He's confused now," I report. "Thinks maybe you'll throw him another curve."

"Fastball, up," Jake suggests.

"Go for it, big guy." Strike three! Attaboy, lover!

Not as mobile as I'd like to be, I remain by the mound when Durham takes the field. The Bulls' pitcher's musings are coming in loud and clear.

"See if you can tell me what he's gonna throw," Jake

suggests, before heading into the dugout at the end of the eighth. It doesn't take long to figure what he has in mind.

As the Clippers bat in the top of the ninth, Jake sidles up to Brendan Baker on the dugout bench. The twenty-two-year-old, left-handed first baseman is the Clippers' best hitter. More importantly, he's the third batter of the inning. Though the two barely know each other, Baker's already figured a few things out about my man. First, he knows that Jake, eleven years his senior, has been around the block. Second, he figures a graduate of Stanford and Harvard might know a thing or two more than a kid who squeezed through high school by the skin of his teeth. So, when Jake offers advice, Baker's inclined to listen—even if Jake *is* just a pitcher. Besides, the kid's fanned three times already and can use all the help he can get.

"I think I can work out what the pitcher's gonna throw you," Jake tells Baker. He spits onto the dugout floor to emphasize the point and lend it baseball cred.

Have you ever wondered why baseball players spit like they've contracted mad cow disease? Now, I know. Because there's nothing to stop them: there are no women in the dugout to complain, and they play on a field where slobber's good for the turf. Basketball players, on the other hand, would slip and break their necks. For the gridiron crowd, hocking through helmets is counterproductive. Imagine a field full of fat guys with sticky strands of drool hanging from their faceguards all afternoon. Just saying.

Jake runs through a simple set of signals he can use to convey to Brendan the pitches we expect he'll be thrown. With the Clippers' dugout on the third-base side, Jake's signals will be easily visible to Baker from the left-hand batter's box. "You game?" he asks the young slugger after he lays out the plan.

"What've I got to lose?" Baker says. Not as dumb as he looks.

After the first two Clippers' batters are retired, Brendan steps up to the plate. He glances at the signals from the third-base coach—a mere formality. Then he peers at Jake on the dugout steps.

"Curve, away," I tell Jake, confirming the pitcher's read of the catcher's sign. Jake gives Brendan the corresponding signal. As expected, the pitch is low and away, and Brendan lays off.

"Fastball, up," I say. Jake signals accordingly. Again, Brendan lets it pass—a fastball well above the strike zone.

Baker steps out of the box. "Fuckin' a—," he says to himself, "how does grandpa know this shit?" Brendan's brimming with confidence as he returns to the plate.

"Fastball, away," I say. Jake relays the sign with a subtle shake of his head. The pitch is just what the doctor ordered, right in Brendan's wheelhouse. He lays into it, taking it to the opposite field with every ounce of his being, the bat connecting with a *thump* that echoes through the park. The ball keeps rising, heading for the top of the thirty-two-foot wall they call The Blue Monster. As the Clippers leap to the top step of the dugout for a better view, the ball clears the wall, striking the scrotum of the mammoth sheet metal bull above it, immediately below the sign that reads "Hit Bull, Win Steak." Although it's not supposed to happen unless a Durham hitter accomplishes the feat, the bull's eyes flash bright red, its tail wags, and a puff of smoke spews from its nostrils, as Brendan jogs triumphantly around the bases.

My widower and I retire the Bulls in order in the bottom of the ninth, sealing a stirring 1-0 victory for darling Jake. I'm having the time of my death!

Two hours later, a local steakhouse makes good on its promise, treating Brendan and his special guest, Jake Singer, to a pair of porterhouse steaks. I decide to tag along.

"How the hell did you know what was coming?" Brendan asks, savoring a forkful of tender, red meat.

"My dead wife told me," Jake answers, smiling.

Brendan laughs. "That's crazy, old man."

"You've got that right."

CHAPTER FORTY-THREE

Jake

On Wednesday, two days after my Clippers' debut, Chris Latham beckons me into his office before our game in Allentown. Once a heralded Indians' prospect, the Clippers' skipper reached The Show briefly, enjoying the proverbial "cup of coffee" for a few short weeks in '97.

"What's up, Skip?" I ask, hopefully.

"Indians need a starter in San Diego on Saturday night." He pauses for effect. "You're it, Jake. You're going to The Show."

These were the words I'd longed to hear since Little League. I stand there, mouth agape, speechless. I remember the good times, my triumphs at Stanford, Lowell, and Trenton. I recall the bitter disappointments: the torn ligament in my elbow, the bizarre attack that severed a finger and stifled a dream. Tears form in the corners of my eyes as I struggle to find my voice.

"Ain't no cryin' in baseball, Singer. Yah know that, right?"

"I know that, Skip," I say, trying mightily to retain my composure.

Latham smiles broadly. "I remember the feeling. Hope you make a bigger splash than I did." He reaches out to shake my hand. "I'm rootin' for ya. We all are." He returns to his game face. "You report Friday. Now, get the hell out of my fucking clubhouse!"

It takes only moments for my teammates to pick up on the

vibe. It's a sixth sense. Guys on the way up have seen my look on other faces, and guys who've been there before recall how they felt. A murmur rises to a crescendo of congratulations, back-slapping, hand-shaking, and good wishes, as I empty my locker into my gym bag and prepare to leave. This is what it's like to be a member of the baseball fraternity; I've known these guys for all of two days, but it seems like forever.

She waits until I reach the hotel. The moment I shut the door to my room, she's in my head. Have you ever heard a dead woman scream? It's otherworldly. Kate's beside herself, metaphorically speaking. Had she been alive at that moment, she'd have leapt into my arms like Yogi Berra did with Don Larsen after Larsen's perfect game in the 1956 World Series. She's delirious with excitement.

"Easy, Kate, you'll wet your pants!"

"As if!" she laughs. I can picture the smile that might have accompanied her laughter, if she'd still been alive. Much as I appreciate her posthumous affection, I long at this moment to hold her in my arms, to feel her warmth and joy. It aches that I can't.

"So, when do we leave?" she asks.

"We?" Kate has accompanied me this far on my quest. I guess it's only fair that she finish the journey.

"Look, Jake," she says, a hint of concern in her voice. "It's a long way from Allentown to San Diego. It wasn't easy to get to Akron or Durham—or for that matter, here to Allentown. What if I don't make it to San Diego? I've got no idea how far these crazy teleportation skills will take me."

"Fly with me," I suggest. I'm offering a ghost a piggyback trip on Delta. "Will that work?"

"Damned if I know, but it's worth a try."

"Can you make it through airport security?"

"X-rays of my head will show nothing," she jokes.

"Seems to me I've heard that one before." It was what wacky Hall-of-Fame pitcher Dizzy Dean told reporters after he'd been hit in the head while breaking up a double play during the 1934 World Series. It takes on a more literal meaning with Kate.

I call my parents. It's the best news they've heard from me in a long while. Dad's thrilled to make the two-hour drive from Newport Beach to attend my debut; Mom will join him, giving her mice a well-deserved breather.

Next, I telephone Nick. He, too, is ecstatic. The drive from Tucson is six hours, but he "wouldn't miss it for the world," he tells me.

"Will you bring Trudy?"

"Don't know," he says, "she hates the long ride."

"No problem." I offer to leave him two tickets, just in case. "How's Christie holding up?" I ask.

"Working her buns off, but no problems we can't handle."

"Will you give her the news?"

"Of course." I wonder if I should call her directly, invite her to come. But I decide against it, fearing it presumptuous.

I don't call Lorna. But she reads the papers. She knows I'll be starting on Saturday, and her weekends are free. She calls me on my cell, vowing to be there. "Can you leave me a ticket?" she asks.

"Sure," I say, before considering the consequences.

CHAPTER FORTY-FOUR

Jake

It takes all day Thursday to fly from Allentown to San Diego. I worry that I'll lose Kate during the connection in Detroit, but she manages to stick with me. We communicate primarily in the on-board rest rooms, where no one can hear me carry on an animated conversation with a ghost.

When I arrive at San Diego's Petco Park on Friday afternoon, I'm greeted by a horde of reporters. This, for me, is a first. I hadn't spent enough time in Akron or Columbus to get noticed, but here I am at a road venue and the Cleveland media is all over me. Indians' manager Marty Milano hears the commotion outside the clubhouse door and swoops in to rescue me. "He'll talk with you later, boys," he tells the media congregation, yanking me by the arm and dragging me into the sanctuary of the clubhouse.

"Let's chat in my office," he says.

Milano, as any Tucsonan will know, played his college ball at the University of Arizona, leading the Wildcats to a College World Series championship and garnering the Golden Spikes Award as the premier college baseball player in the country. He went on to a relatively lackluster ten-year major league career followed by stints as manager of the Phillies, Red Sox, and now, the Cleveland Indians. Just over six feet tall, he's known for his shaved head, impish smile, and garrulous nature.

"Welcome aboard," he says. "I'm Marty Milano." He motions me to a chair across from his desk. "Harley McGinniss thinks you're the cat's meow."

"We go back almost twenty years," I say, "when he scouted me in high school in Southern California."

Though interrupted constantly by players, coaches, trainers, and other assorted team personnel, Marty extracts from me a brief summary of my unconventional path to the major leagues. We compare notes about Tucson. He listens intently to everything I tell him.

"Hey, listen, kid. Harley told me about losing your wife. Really sorry to hear that."

"I feel as if she's still with me," I reply.

"That's nice," Marty says. He pauses a respectful few moments before resuming. "Okay, I don't know what you might've been expecting, but the media's already sniffed you out. Not every day a thirty-three-year-old rookie with a Harvard Law degree pops into a major league dugout. So, I'd suggest you go and sit down with those fellas in the media room straight off. Answer their questions. They're a pretty decent lot. And it's the Cleveland press, not the Boston or New York writers, so they're not gonna be too hard on you. Best to make their acquaintance—they've got a job to do, just like you do."

"Appreciate the warm welcome," I say, before he leads me into the den of wolves.

It would be hard to overstate the media fascination with a thirty-three-year-old left-handed rookie with a mangled left hand, degrees from Stanford and Harvard, a ten-year layoff, and a recently deceased wife. The questions are endless, and sometimes bizarre. You can hear a pin drop when I relate the saga of my missing digit.

"Incredible!" chirps a reporter for Channel 4 News.

"You couldn't *make* this shit up!" croaks a sportswriter for the *Cleveland Plain Dealer*.

"My editor won't believe a word of this." And so on.

"How does that Harvard law degree help you on the mound?" asks a television reporter, hoping for a juicy quote.

"If I can't strike 'em out, I can sue 'em," I quip. They like that one.

"Word is you talk to yourself on the mound. Is that right, Jake?" asks a radio reporter who's done his homework. I decide it couldn't hurt to be candid.

"To be honest, I talk to my wife. I know it sounds silly, but I think she's there for me in some way I can't really explain."

"Good one, Jake." Kate interjects. "Maybe you can have them interview me. You can act as my medium. That oughta blow their minds."

"You must miss her terribly," the lone female reporter chimes in.

"If you only knew," I say, suppressing a smile.

Word of my arrival—and backstory—filters rapidly through the Indians' clubhouse. While some players are intrigued, others resent the attention accorded an unproven rookie. On balance, my Harvard Law degree is a liability. Most have scant respect for lawyers, though no compunction about soliciting free legal advice on everything from contract negotiations to marital issues. The first hint of friction comes in the initial meeting with my new pitching coach, Judd Masters, and Silvio Garcia, the talented young receiver who'll catch my start tomorrow night.

Masters is a former major league pitcher. Bright, articulate, and opinionated, he's only eight years my senior. Garcia, a two-time All-Star at twenty-nine, is a brash Dominican who takes as much pride in his defensive capabilities as he does in his hitting prowess. What they don't know, as we meet to develop a game plan, is that there are actually *four* of us in the room.

"You're wet behind the ears," Masters begins, "so we're gonna make this as easy as possible." He rubs his nose thoughtfully. "Silvio here caught last night's game and has been through the Padres' scouting reports. He knows their tendencies. He's gonna call your game. He'll assess what you've got in the first inning or two and go with your strengths. Now, that's pretty damn easy, right?"

"Who the fuck does this guy think he is?" Kate exclaims.

"Calm down," I mutter, without thinking.

"What did you say?" asks Masters, sensing resistance.

"Sorry, I've got a tendency to talk to myself at times," I explain.

"So I hear," Masters says.

"Thing is, I've got a system that works for me," I say, as respectfully as possible. "I'm pretty good at anticipating what batters expect."

"That's Silvio's job. He knows these guys better than you do."

"I respect that, but I'm not really comfortable unless I'm calling my own game." I can almost see the steam escaping from their nostrils, like human versions of the Durham bull.

"That's my hero," Kate pipes up. "Stand your ground, lover!"

"Jesus Christ!" Masters barks. "You think that fucking degree from Harvard makes you smarter than everyone else?"

"Shit, yeah!" Kate interjects.

"It's not that at all," I plead.

"Fookin' rookie!" Garcia sneers, the first words he's uttered since the meeting began. He promptly stands up and walks out.

"Do what you want, asshole," Masters says. He follows Garcia out the door. "It's your career."

CHAPTER FORTY-FIVE

Kate

We're perusing the scouting reports on the Padres' hitters late Saturday morning when someone raps on the door of Jake's hotel room.

"Expecting someone?" I ask Jake.

"Nope. Why don't you go answer it?"

"You're a riot."

Jake walks to the door. He glances through the peephole. "Oh, shit," he moans. "I don't have time for this."

I don't have to wait for him to tell me who it is. Sure as I'm dead, it's Big Red.

"Surprise!" She stands at the open door, dressed like a horny teenager in tight jeans and a halter-top. Come to think of it, that's how I dressed for my first date with Jake at Antonio's Pizzeria back in Cambridge four years ago. Jake relieved me of that outfit just a few hours later, as I recall.

"Lorna!" Jake sputters. "I wasn't expecting to see you before tonight's game." The overnight bag lying on the floor beside her is hard to overlook.

"Been driving since six this morning," she says. "Wanted to catch you before you left for the ballpark, to wish you luck."

"How did you know where to find me?"

"The team hotels are listed on the internet." No one said she wasn't resourceful. She pauses, staring at Jake. "Gonna invite me in?"

"Sure, sure, Lorna, come on in."

I'm a gal, or at least I was one. I know what machinations are going on inside her pretty little red head before I even begin to pierce her thoughts. Show up looking like a tasty cherry popsicle with luggage and he'll *have* to invite you to stay the night. Well, this isn't gonna happen if I have anything to say about it!

"Tell that fake carrot-topped floozy that you've got scouting reports to review! This is the most important game of your life! No time for fucking around, Jake," I scold him.

Jake's mind is spinning. Most of him knows I'm right. But the part below his belt operates on a different frequency, and Lorna's dressed for maximum appeal to that frequency.

Lorna enters the room, rolling her bag behind her, while Jake stands helplessly by, unsure what to do. She puts the bag down and reaches out to embrace him, kissing him hard on the lips. Smooth move. This is going to be a challenge.

"Uh, look Lorna, I'd really like to spend time with you, but I have to prepare for the game." He gestures toward the bed, strewn with scouting reports. "I've got reports to go through, and then I've got to get over to the park early and—"

Lorna flashes a fake pout, female code for *okay, if we can't screw now, I'll come back after the game tonight, and we'll fuck like bunnies 'til the morning light.* "I understand," she says. "Sorry, I should have realized you'd have more important things to do." She looks at him with doe eyes. "Tried to book a room for the night here, but they're full. Know of any . . ."

Before I can even open my non-existent mouth, Jake capitulates . . . completely. "Leave your bag here. I'll call the front desk and ask them to issue you a key card. I need about an hour more alone here and then I'll go to the park. You can use the room this afternoon if you like and meet me here tonight after the game."

"Goddammit, Jake!" I say, my spectral volume turned up to the max.

"You're a dear, Jake," she says, cooing like a pigeon.

CHAPTER FORTY-SIX

Jake

I don't know what to do about Lorna, but I can't waste precious time and energy pondering that problem before the most important game of my life.

There are only a handful of players in the clubhouse when I enter Petco Park at one o'clock. I'm unaccustomed to the luxury of major league facilities—even the visitors' clubhouse is decked out like a yacht. A spread of cold cuts, fruits, pizza, barbecued chicken, breads, and every conceivable non-alcoholic beverage is laid out on a table at the far end of the room. I grab a bite before the head trainer beckons me to the training room. Twenty minutes of heat on my left elbow and shoulder is followed by ultrasound for my deltoids and rotator cuff. He finishes me off with a quick massage and some stretching. It feels more like a resort spa than an athletic training room.

I spend my next hour going over hitting charts with the bullpen coach. Judd Masters, still smarting from the perceived snub from his smart-ass rookie pitcher, keeps his distance, although Silvio Garcia stops by later to share his thoughts on the Padres' lineup. When he finishes, he returns to the sticky subject of yesterday's meeting.

"So, Rook, ya gonna leet me call your game . . . or no?

"Let's play it by ear, Silvio."

He smirks. "You da boss," he says. "It ain't gonna be *my* funeral."

"No, it was mine," Kate squeals.

"Where've you been?" I ask her.

"Nearly fell asleep in that massage parlor."

"It's a training room, Kate. Not sure it's a proper hangout for wives."

"All those hard bodies in there. Could almost feel it in my loins. You know, like an amputee can feel the missing parts?"

"I can't believe we're having this discussion. You're telling me you still get turned on? Really, Kate?"

"Yeah, I guess so. Maybe we should try something . . . sort of like phone sex, maybe. Whaddya think, Jakie?"

"Absolutely not! Jesus, Kate, you're incorrigible!"

"Not a clue what that means, but thank you, Jake."

The buzz around the ballpark grows steadily as game time approaches. Local publicity about the four-fingered freak rookie pitcher who talks to himself on the mound bloats the attendance. I'd pitched before twenty thousand or so at Omaha during the 2001 College World Series, but word is that the Saturday-night crowd could double that.

While my new teammates stop by to wish me luck, it's Marty Milano's visit that helps the most. Marty strolls over and sits beside me on the bench while the Indians bat in the top of the first inning.

"Hey, kid. You nervous?" he asks.

"Yeah, a little bit."

"That's just the right amount. Listen, kid," he says, "you've got some talented ballplayers behind you. You don't need to do it alone. Breathe out there. Enjoy it. You only get one debut, and it ought to be fun, just like it was back in Little League."

"Like the man said," Kate adds, "you won't be alone. I'm here for you, lover."

The Indians go down quickly in the first. I feel chills as I climb up the dugout steps and onto the field. I've waited my whole life for this. I try to think positively, to think, as Marty urged, like a Little Leaguer. As I complete my warm-ups, Kate tries to calm me.

"Remember what Yogi said. Baseball's ninety percent mental, and the other half, physical," Kate says. "So, between us, we've got it made." I don't know what it means, but I appreciate the thought.

Speedy veteran Donny Bracken is the Padres' first hitter. About my age, he broke into pro ball about the same time I did. He's been with five teams in the interceding years; I've been with two law firms.

Silvio calls for a fastball, low and away.

"Kate?" I ask.

"I'm good," she replies. What the fuck does that mean?

I throw the fastball, but it drifts over the heart of the plate. Bracken slaps it through the left side for a single. An inauspicious start.

"I thought you were here for me, Kate. What's going on?"

"Houston, we have a problem," she says.

"What the fuck does *that* mean?"

"Too much noise in the stadium. It's like static. I'm having trouble connecting with the batter's thoughts."

Fuck me.

Next up is the center fielder, Chris Campbell. Silvio crouches, plunging his right hand between his legs. He thrusts a pinkie in the direction of first base: the sign for a pickoff. I nod, go into my stretch. I stop, spin, and fire to first, just as

Bracken bolts for second. Travis Bates, our burly first baseman, scoops up my low throw and heaves the ball toward second. It soars *way* over the head of the shortstop, high enough to threaten low-flying aircraft. When the dust clears, Bracken stands at third base. I've still only thrown one pitch.

Judd Masters pokes his head out of the dugout, calls time, and jogs to the mound. Silvio flips off his mask and scampers out to join us.

"Look, kid. It's no big deal," Judd says. "Forget about Bracken at third. Just focus on the batter. Throw what Silvio tells you to throw."

Silvio deposits a glob of sputum on the mound, right in my landing spot. "C'mon, rook!" he mutters, running off to resume his position behind the plate.

Campbell steps back into the batter's box. Silvio orders a slider, low and away.

"Kate?"

"Still nothing," she says.

The slider yields a swing-and-miss, my first major league strike. Silvio calls for an inside fastball.

"Stee-rike two!" bellows the umpire.

The next two offerings are fastballs away, waste pitches designed to tempt the batter while setting him up for something to finish him off. Silvio orders the curveball.

"No!" Kate howls. "He's looking for the curveball! Throw him your change!" I shake Silvio off. Stubbornly, he puts down the same sign again. Again, I shake him off.

"Fookin' time out!" Silvio springs from his crouch and dashes toward the mound. "What the fook, rook?" he wails.

"He's looking for the curve," I tell him.

"Woops, now he's thinking fastball," Kate says, reversing course.

"Sorry, fastball," I correct myself.

Silvio shakes his head in frustration. "First you tells me he's lookin' curve, then you tells me he's lookin' fasball!"

"He changed his mind," I explain. Silvio groans. I insist on throwing my changeup.

"Your fookin' funeral," Silvio says, replacing his mask and stomping back to the plate.

"I wish he'd stop saying that," Kate complains.

Primed for the heater, Campbell whiffs on the changeup. It's my first big league strikeout. Silvio lifts his mask, propelling a thick stream of saliva in front of home plate. Had it been a Hallmark card, it would have read "fook you, rook, you were lucky."

"How're you doing, Kate," I ask.

"Coming in clearer now," she says. "Like tuning in a radio."

With the runner on third, I stay on Kate's frequency. I induce a pair of lazy infield pop-outs to end the inning.

We take the lead in the second on a solo shot by Bates. "Payback for that little flub in the first," he snickers as he descends the dugout steps after completing his home run trot.

"Might wanna throw away a few more," I suggest, never dreaming he'd take me seriously.

In the top of the third, I bat for the first time since high school. We're in a National League Park where there's no designated hitter. Marty sidles up to me as I grab a bat from the bat rack.

"Know what to do what that thing?" he asks me, a smirk plastered between the parentheses of his puffy cheeks.

"Been a while," I admit.

"Well, you just let it sit on your shoulder," he commands me. "I don't want you pulling a muscle tryin' to be a hero. You swing that piece a lumber and your night's over, got it?"

I can see from the look in his eyes that he's serious. So I do what he says. I stand at the plate like a department store mannequin and strike out looking.

Kate and I work our way through the next few innings, accommodating Silvio whenever we can. But when Kate feels strongly about a batter's expectations, I defer to my secret weapon.

By now, my penchant for on-mound conversation is apparent to everyone. Sonny Graham, our veteran third baseman, just shakes his head and smiles. Dan Murphy, our center fielder, asks if I'm reciting Shakespeare. "Who's Kate?" asks shortstop Larry Wagner.

"Probably misheard me," I tell him. "Said *plate.* Reminding myself to get the ball over the *plate.*"

"Nice save," Kate says.

Heading out for the bottom of the seventh, I've already thrown eighty-five pitches. I figure it's my last inning.

"Roger that," says Kate, after boring into the thoughts of our skipper. "He really likes you, Jake," she adds.

But things get hairy in the seventh. I begin by walking Bracken. Campbell flies out harmlessly to right. Wendell Hill's up next.

"Bracken's running on the next pitch," Kate warns me. I shake off Silvio repeatedly until, supremely annoyed, he thrusts out his pinkie for the pickoff. I pivot and fire to first, just as Bracken takes off. Bates snatches it cleanly. This time, he hurls it into the stratosphere. Laughing, Bracken scampers to third.

"My bad!" shouts Bates, though he doesn't seem too troubled. His second blunder of the night costs a run when Bracken scores on Hill's sacrifice fly. I strike out the next hitter on three pitches, shaking off my befuddled receiver six times.

"You one fookin' pain in the ass," Silvio says, as we jog off the diamond, the score knotted at one after seven innings.

Milano shuffles over to me as I enter the dugout, extending his hand. "Great game, kid," he says, his big grin distended by the enormous wad of bubblegum lodged in his right cheek. "We'll take it from here." Following his lead, the whole dugout marches by, smacking me on the rump, high-fiving me, or shaking my hand. It's like a reception line after an open bar. The last one by is Judd Masters.

"You are one fucking unconventional pitcher, Jake Singer," he says, shaking his head as a reluctant smile creeps onto his face. "Pitch like that, and you can do things any fucking way you want."

The postscript is simple. In the top of the eighth, atoning for his second error, Travis Bates reprises his earlier home run with a two-run shot. Relievers shut down the Padres in the eighth and ninth to preserve my first major league victory. How sweet it is.

CHAPTER FORTY-SEVEN

Kate

I've never been prouder of Jake. I want so badly to take him into my arms and squeeze him, but he's too busy handling the congratulations of his teammates and the fawning questions of the press. And, as the record will show, I no longer have arms.

After he's showered and dressed in the clubhouse, Jake greets his proud parents, Nick, and, much to his surprise and apparent delight, Christie, who'd accepted Nick's offer to drive out with him for the game. Christie, of course, has no way of knowing that the flamboyant redhead in the row behind her was anticipating a carnal rendezvous with our hero later that evening. All but Lorna join Jake for a drink at the hotel bar. Big Red bows out early and heads upstairs to prep for a night of grunting like a javelina in heat.

Jake arranges to meet his parents and Nick for breakfast before they leave town; Christie's unavailable, having made plans to visit friends before flying home late Sunday night. But she gladly accepts Jake's invitation to join him for dinner after Sunday afternoon's game.

Between the demands of the media and the time spent with family and friends, it's two a.m. when Jake returns to the room. I've been babysitting Big Red, though she's none the wiser. Dressed in a provocative black negligee, she spends most of that time in the bathroom, gussying herself up, applying just the right amount of makeup, a shade of lipstick (she'd brought three sticks, applying and removing two before settling on Candy Apple Red), brushing that long, fake-red hair, and dabbing enough perfume in strategic locations (including, of course, her *not*-red, well-manicured pubic triangle) to anesthetize a horse. The entire room smells like a perfume insert in the Sunday newspaper. That I could smell without a nose was no stranger than any other aspect of my baffling existence.

Poor Lorna. She'd been up at five in the morning, on the road by six. She'd driven six hard hours across the Arizona desert and over the mountains east of San Diego. It was no wonder then, that despite her best efforts to remain conscious, she falls into a deep sleep just minutes before Jake's arrival.

Jake, too, is exhausted after an eventful day. He elects to let Lorna sleep, brushing his teeth quietly in the bathroom before undressing and slipping under the covers beside her. I say nothing, remembering that I'm not particularly welcome in the presence of Jake's lady friends.

Lorna is the first to stir as the morning sun creeps around the edges of the drawn window shades. She gasps, realizing that her preparations the night before had been for naught. She rolls over, aiming her ample breasts toward Jake, who now begins to stir. He opens his gorgeous blue-gray eyes and smiles warily.

"Guess I fell asleep before you got back," she says. "I'm so sorry, Jake." But Jake isn't sorry; in fact, he's relieved. A wild night of sex would have been nice, he figures, but would have made it more awkward to say what he's resolved to say this morning. I keep quiet, sensing that he doesn't need coaching.

"It's okay, Lorna." She's about to lean over to kiss him when he draws back.

"What's wrong?" she asks. "Am I still competing with Kate?"

"You could never compete with me, Red!" I blurt out. Shit. Couldn't help myself. Jake grimaces slightly, but elects to ignore me.

"This is never going to work, Lorna," Jake says.

"Why not?" Her voice betrays her devastation.

"Because we've built this on physical attraction and convenience," he begins, meeting her gaze. "I'm at a crossroads. Don't know if I'm a lawyer or a baseball player. Don't know where I'll be or what I'll be doing three months from now, much less beyond that. I'm living my life like I've never lived it before—day by day." Jake sits up, resting his back against his pillow. "You're looking for a surrogate father for your four kids. You're young, you're beautiful, but I'm not in the market for an instant family. Do you understand what I'm trying to say?"

Lorna's Candy-Apple-Red lips tremble. In her mind, she sees herself with the inside track on a dynamic athlete or talented lawyer—it doesn't matter which—a dreamboat who can free her from the shackles of a humdrum existence raising four rambunctious kids, and help her avoid the bottle that's become her only refuge since the shock of a horrible divorce. She's understandably shattered.

"I have to go," she says, turning toward the bathroom, her voice unsteady.

Jake feels like a cad. "Are you okay?" he asks her.

"No, but I will be." She sighs deeply. "I hope."

I feel sorry for Big Red. Silently, we watch her pack her things, dress hurriedly, and exit room 514.

"Better not hear an 'I told you so,'" Jake warns.

"You did the right thing," I reply. "But she couldn't compete with me, could she, Jake?"

"No, Kate," Jake says, grinning. "You're one of a kind."

CHAPTER FORTY-EIGHT

Jake

I sit alone at a quiet table along the back wall of the trendy Italian restaurant off the hotel lobby. As I await Christie's arrival, my mind is adrift in a vortex of emotions. I consider my intentions and wonder if my courage will match my resolve.

My relationship with Christie is fraught with complexity and constraint. It's more than a collaboration between colleagues. She's my friend and confidante. She was there for me during the darkest days of my marriage, selflessly offering advice and reassurance. We've acknowledged our mutual admiration, but treaded no further. The spark between us might have grown into a raging fire, but we resisted the temptation, scrupulously maintaining the purely professional relationship mandated by the norms of the workplace. We joked about those restraints—she dubbed them "Nick's Decrees of Separation." Pretty clever, I thought.

If Christie bears any animus toward me for leaving her to fend for herself at DD&S, it didn't prevent her from traveling six hours to witness my debut, or from accepting my invitation to dinner. But why did she agree to come? To solicit work advice? To address the awkwardness between us since Kate's death? Will her presence signal a willingness to confront the unexpressed feelings we might harbor for each other? Do our goals and desires conflict or align?

Christie flashes a radiant smile as the hostess leads her to our table. She wears a white, Western-style shirt with embroidered sleeves over a sleek pair of designer jeans. And just for me, she dons a dark blue Cleveland Indians' baseball cap with a red brim and the Indians' traditional red-faced Chief Wahoo logo on the crest.

"Pretty racist, don't you think?" she says, grimacing as she points to her headgear. "Almost didn't buy it. But it was the only one they had in the souvenir shop. Twenty-eight bucks for the right to blithely offend Native Americans! Can you believe it?" She promptly removes the cap, depositing it on the floor with her pocketbook.

"Well, I appreciate the gesture," I laugh, "if not the logo." Her presence buoys me, particularly in the wake of the fiasco that morning with Lorna. "Glad you could come. We didn't really have a chance to talk last night."

"Last night was your night," she says. "And rightfully so." She lifts the folded cloth napkin from the table and places it neatly upon her lap.

To salute my triumph, Christie insists on treating us to a bottle of champagne. It's a generous and thoughtful gesture.

I begin the conversation by apologizing for the burdens imposed by my abrupt departure.

"Chance of a lifetime," she responds. "Couldn't have been happier for you."

"I appreciate that, Christie," I say, as I dip into the bubbly. "How about Nick? Is he still pissed off at me?"

"If he is, he hasn't shown it, especially last night. He was euphoric. Like he was fifteen." She takes a first sip of champagne. "Gave me a crash course in pitching philosophy." She laughs. "As enlightening as it was tedious."

"He's been like that since the day we met at Stanford," I chuckle.

She orders the pasta puttanesca, while I opt for the veal Milanese. Until the arrival of our entrées, we savor the champagne and talk shop. Her efficiency and attention to detail comfort and impress me, as they always have.

The meals arrive and we dig in. She fills me in on office gossip, we rail against Arizona politics, and I regale her with tales from the clubhouse. The waiter clears our plates and we order dessert.

I decide that the time has come. I drain what remains of the champagne as fortification. "Can we talk about the elephant in the room?"

"Your way of intimating that I've put on weight?"

"Hardly," I laugh. "You look stunning." I pause, still mustering my courage. There's no way I'm turning back now.

"Christie," I ask, "how would you react . . . if I leaned over this table . . . and kissed you?"

She smiles broadly. "I'd be delighted." Best possible answer.

"And if I ripped off my shirt and embraced you?"

"I'd call hotel security." We both laugh.

"You know, Kate had always been jealous of you. When things went south between us, she was convinced we were having an affair. God knows I was tempted, particularly that night at the hotel in Flagstaff. But I'm not that impulsive . . . or reckless."

"Until now," she says, grinning. The waiter comes by with espressos, a generous square of tiramisu, and a pair of forks. "I think you know that I wouldn't have reciprocated," she says. "I had too much respect for you . . . and for Kate."

"There is no more Kate," I say, even though it's a debatable premise. I made Kate swear, spook's honor, not to attend this dinner.

"Are you sure?" She looks at me dubiously. "Nick's convinced that you haven't quite let her go . . . that you still . . . *converse* with her on occasion."

Although Nick has obviously let the cat—the Kate?—out of the bag, I choose to neither confirm nor deny it. "We all have our ways of coping, Christie," I say, evasively. "What if it were true?"

"You're entitled to your memories, Jake," she says, delicately sipping her espresso, "but I've no interest in competing with—"

"A ghost?" I say, sparing her the need to complete the sentence. She nods, biting her lip. "My marriage was . . . complicated. So is my grief. But no, I wouldn't expect you, or anyone, to compete with Kate." I wonder if Kate would concur.

We finish our espressos while we demolish the tiramisu.

"Would you like to see Cleveland some weekend in September, when the Indians are home, after I get settled in?"

"Paris on the Cuyahoga? What girl could resist?"

"We'll go to the Rock and Roll Hall of Fame. Afterward, we can light a fire on the river and watch it burn." She laughs. I reach out and grasp her hand. She squeezes back gently and smiles.

"What about Nick's Decrees of Separation?" she says. "I could sue you for sexual harassment."

"Innocent, your honor. At least so far."

CHAPTER FORTY-NINE

Kate

I'm the dead wife of a celebrity!

First, he appeared in a feature on ESPN's *SportsCenter*, then on all three of the major national news reports. "Four-Finger" Singer, winner of the first *five* of his major league starts after a decade-long layoff. Unheard of!

Heartthrob! That was the headline of the piece on *Entertainment Tonight*. "Handsome, talented, educated at Stanford and Harvard, Jake Singer is the sports world's most eligible bachelor," gushed co-anchor Nancy O'Dell. Even *I* got airtime! "Barely four-and-a-half months after the tragic death of his beautiful wife, Kate, Cleveland Indians' lefthander Jake Singer is setting the sports world abuzz!" I don't know where they got those photos of me, but they appeared everywhere, on television, in newspapers, and magazines. The headshot wasn't bad. But the other one was positively scandalous! It was a photo taken back in 2010, me in my "eye patch" bikini, taken on that first visit to Jake's parents' Newport Beach house. Did Jake's *Dad* release that? Is it possible to fall in love with your former self? God, I so miss that body!

How do I know all this nonsense? Creative use of my 'dead time.' I hang around bars, restaurants—wherever I can find a TV. At first, I piggybacked on Jake's television regimen. But consuming a steady diet of *SportsCenter* and the MLB Network was killing me. On occasion, when he felt unusually charitable, he'd flip on one of my favorite programs, before heading off to do something else. But I don't push my luck. "I'm not your damn remote control," he warns me. Actually, he is.

And then came the stories about Jake's "mound antics." Slow-motion close-ups seemed to confirm he'd been talking to *me* on the mound. Imagine that! I soon became the most famous deceased wife in sports history!

No, Jake didn't deny it. When we realized he'd been 'outed' as a dead wife whisperer, we devised an appropriate strategy.

"I'm just gonna admit it, Kate," he told me a day before an interview with *60 Minutes* correspondent Scott Pelley. "What's so horrible about a recent widower seeking inspiration and consolation from his recently deceased wife?"

"That's fine," I said, "as long as you don't admit she talks back . . . or reads minds . . . or makes pitch suggestions, or—"

"Or teleports. Or interferes in my love life. Or—"

"Okay, already! The more you reveal, the crazier *you* sound, right?"

"Right. And I'm clearly not crazy, am I Kate?"

"Of course not." I hesitated. "I don't think so." I paused again. "Probably not." Another pause. "Maybe you are. You talk with your dead wife, for God's sake."

I'm pleased for Jake. I really am. He's living his dream. But there's this recurrent nightmare that I worry about. That prick, Billy Garabedian. Now that Jake's a household name, will Billy crawl out of some hole and sell that porno flick to some sleazy website or publication, sullying my reputation forever? I, too, am a celebrity now. I could never have imagined the attention I'm receiving. To turn it into something shameful would be devastating, both to Jake and to me. I can't let that happen.

After giving the matter considerable thought, I decide on preemptive action.

According to Jake, Billy pleaded guilty to extortion. He began an eighteen-month sentence in July. A mere slap on the wrist! With time off for good behavior, Jake said, chances are he'll be out in a year.

Thus far, I've been an exemplary ghost. Like Casper the Friendly Ghost, or the Ghost of Christmas Past. But now, it's time to rewrite the script, become the classic, bone-chilling poltergeist. Do I have it in me? You bet I do.

CHAPTER FIFTY

Jake

It's the afternoon following my fifth consecutive victory, over the Angels in Anaheim. I'm in the visitors' training room, icing my left elbow, when my cell phone rings.

"Jake Singer?" a female voice inquires.

"Who is this?" Almost nobody has my cell phone number—only my parents, Nick, Christie, and, of course, Kate, who has neither need for a cell phone nor digits to dial with.

"This is Elaine Davis, agent for Madelyn Moss," she says.

"Who's Madelyn Moss, and how did you get my number?"

Travis Bates, in the midst of treatment on his ailing hamstring, snaps to attention when he hears the name. "Jesus, Singer, you fucking live under a rock?"

There's momentary silence on the other end of the line—disbelief, perhaps, over my lack of recognition. Just as I'm about to hang up, she identifies her client as "one of Hollywood's hottest starlets," and proceeds to explain why she's called. "Miss Moss grew up in Ohio, is a big fan of the Indians, and very much wants to meet you."

"Madelyn Moss wants to meet me?"

Bates lunges off the table. He snatches the phone from my grip. "Sure thing!" he blurts into the phone over my expletive-laden objection. He gathers the details while I wrestle the phone from his grasp.

"Dammit, Travis!" I scream as I regain possession. "Hello?" She's already hung up.

"Chill, rookie," he says. "She says you can meet Madelyn at midnight tonight, at the Tropicana Bar on Hollywood Boulevard."

I'm furious with Bates over his sophomoric stunt. "What in the world possessed you to do that?"

"Jesus, Singer, are you fucking serious?" He looks at me like I'm an alien. "Madelyn Moss is the hottest chick in Hollywood and she wants to meet you. *You*, asshole! Only a crazy moron would turn down an offer like that!"

Possibly crazy, but no moron, I decide to keep the date—mostly to avoid the clubhouse flak I'll endure if I don't. Bates, Garcia, Sonny Graham and three other teammates appoint themselves chaperones.

With a heavy dose of indifference, I arrive with my involuntary entourage at the Roosevelt Hotel in Hollywood just after midnight. As we make our way to its world-famous Tropicana poolside bar, I'm startled by a wave of flashbulbs within a swelling crowd on the other side of the bar.

I stop in my tracks. "I'm not so sure about this," I say to Travis.

Silvio overhears me. "You ain't fookin' backin' out now, rook!" he shouts over the din of the mob. Graham and Garcia each grab an arm and nudge me toward the source of the commotion. Bates takes it upon himself to run interference, driving a wedge into the crowd of hangers-on surrounding the actress.

An older woman, probably Madelyn's agent, spots us immediately. She barks instructions at various subordinates, then sics the photographers on me like a pack of hungry Dobermans. Flashbulbs burst in my face, nearly blinding me.

"Jake Singer, I'm Elaine Davis," she announces. "I'd like you to meet Madelyn Moss." Davis takes me by the arm and ushers me to a beautiful blonde clad in a revealing black gown suitable for the red carpet at the Oscars. She's petite, with narrow hips and cherry lips that part to reveal a bright, toothy smile.

"I'm so glad to meet you, Jake," she purrs in her best Marilyn impression, shaking my hand a little too vigorously.

"It's nice to meet you, too," I say, for lack of anything more original.

"Why don't we pose for a few photos?" Elaine suggests, as if the thought had just popped into her head. Madelyn locks her arm in mine; someone orders us to smile. Flashbulbs assault us, as a growing crowd of gawkers squeals with delight.

After the paparazzi conclude their feeding frenzy, Elaine ushers Madelyn and me through the crowd, away from the bar, through the hotel dining room, and into an empty banquet room. She quickly departs, leaving the two of us alone.

"Sorry about the photographers," Madelyn says. We grab the nearest two chairs. "It's an occupational hazard."

"Don't worry about it, I don't really—"

I'm interrupted by the elaborate ring of her cell phone—a cloying melody I just can't place. She picks up immediately, lifting the phone to her ear.

"Hi, babe," she says, affectionately. She raises her left hand, palm forward, as if invoking time-out from an umpire, then swivels away, prattling on as I sit idly by. Her conversation turns tense, and so do I. Finally, after ten minutes of Hollywood vanity and insolence, I stand up and walk out. She doesn't even notice.

I return to the bar. My entourage is fully engaged with nubile young ladies and plenty of booze. Relieved to be unrecognized, I walk outside, hail a cab, and return to the hotel.

CHAPTER FIFTY-ONE

Billy

I'm counting the fucking days, all 547 of them. Damn lawyer told me if I kept my nose clean, I'd get out in half that time. Could've been worse, he said, much worse. But I had no priors, and nobody knew I was making my living off porn. Told 'em at the sentencing hearing that I'd made the movie for my 'personal gratification,' that times got tough, and, in my desperation, I made a bad choice. Boo hoo! Told that bird-brained fossil of a judge how truly sorry I was. What the fuck! Old bastard didn't give a goddamn shit about me—just another widget on the assembly line. Somebody ticks off a box that says 'eighteen months' and here I rot.

Like I said before, it could be worse. I'm here in no man's land, the Arizona State Prison Complex in San Luis, right smack dab on the Mexican border, a dozen miles south of Yuma. Minimum security, since I didn't beat the shit out of anyone during my 'extortionary escapade,' as my lawyer called it. Lucky, I guess, that Jake Singer didn't beat the shit out of *me*.

And speaking of Jake Singer, I'm watching the news on TV a few nights back, and they're talking about this four-fingered baseball player who comes out of the fucking woodwork—he's some Harvard lawyer, they say—and he's pitching the Cleveland Indians into pennant contention. Well, I don't give a fuck about the Cleveland Indians, but I recognize this asshole right off. I remember that fucked-up hand. They say he's from Tucson, so who else would it be? Then they go on about his *dead* wife. Dead? Kate? No way! So, I go to the prison library and I read about it in a magazine. Hit by a fucking truck! Jesus! She was *so* hot. There's this picture in the magazine where she's wearing a bikini. It's like she's wearing just three fucking postage stamps! My God, what a waste!

Then it hits me. Tabloids, supermarket magazines. I'm thinking *National Enquirer*. They'd pay a pretty penny for a story about Kate Singer. And a fortune for a video or stills! No crime to *sell* that shit to a willing buyer. Who needs extortion?

You don't really think I was stupid enough to destroy all those tapes, do you? And I couldn't give a rat's ass about that paper Jake made me sign. Let the fucker sue me!

So, it's lights out and I'm lying on my cot thinking about how much to ask for my video. An exclusive. *Kate Singer: Porno Queen*. What's it worth? Half a mil? A mil? And I can make all the arrangements from the comfort of my own cozy prison cell!

I'm grinning, dreaming about spending all that scratch, when all of a sudden, from out of fucking nowhere, I hear this voice. A *woman's* voice. There ain't no women's voices in an all-male prison.

"Hey, sleazeball," she says. I jump like a scorpion bit my ass. I hop off my cot, move to the front of my cell. I peer through the bars and into the hallway. It's dark. No movement anywhere. I think to myself: I *know* that voice. And then it fucking hits me. *Kate!* But Kate's pushing daisies. I heard it on TV. I read it right there in that magazine!

"Yeah, sleazeball, it's Kate," says the voice. I smack myself across the cheek. Maybe I'm dreaming. No *maybe* about it; there's no other explanation.

"What the fuck!" I yelp, in what I think is my dream. "Where are you?"

"In your head, jerk-off."

"But you're dead," I say.

"Exactly!"

I circle my cell. Am I nuts? Then it comes to me that someone's stashed a cell phone somewhere. Or one of those miniature speakers. So, I get wise. "Hey, you had me going there," I say, loudly, so I'll be heard by whatever damn fool's out to spook me.

"No, Billy, this isn't some prank." Sure as hell *sounds* like Kate. "I'm deader than a doornail," she yaps, "and you're well on your way to the same fate."

"Prove to me you're really Kate!" I say, refusing to believe the unthinkable. It's too dark to search my cell for electronic devices, but there's gotta be one there, somewhere. I run my fingers under my mattress. Nothing.

"Remember that time at Abe's Diner," the voice says, "when all my tables were full?"

"Wha—"

"You bribed those old ladies to move to another table, so I'd be your waitress. Remember that, Billy?"

I did remember that. Who else could possibly know that?

"You're wondering who else could possibly know that, right, Billy?"

"Uh . . ."

"And you've been thinking about selling that porno to the *National Enquirer*, haven't you, Billy?"

"Never even considered it," I tell her.

"Don't lie to me, Billy. I'm a ghost. I can read your mind."

Okay, so now I'm shaking. Really shaking. I'm talking to a ghost. I mean *really talking to a ghost!* A warm, wet stream trickles into my underwear and down my leg.

"Did I scare the piss out of you, or are you just glad to hear my voice?"

"What do you want?"

"Two possibilities, Billy. You get to choose. Behind one door is retribution. You think life in prison sucks? Choose the door marked 'retribution' and prison will seem like paradise. I'll haunt you day and night until you break, until you can't bear to live with me in your head 24/7. You won't be able to eat or sleep. You'll slam your head against the concrete wall to end your misery. I figure it will take five days, maybe a week at most. I'll have my revenge, you'll have your funeral."

"Okay, so what's behind the second door?" This can't be happening.

"Door Number Two is *way* better . . . and *much, much* worse. You make a solemn promise. And Billy, when I say *solemn*, I mean you're not just making this promise to the ghost of Kate Singer. You're making it to all of Heaven and Hell, so the consequences of breaking that promise will be worse than even you have the capacity to imagine in that twisted brain of yours."

"Promise what?" I'm sweating bullets.

"That you will *never, EVER,* do anything to sully Jake or me, with that video, pictures, *anything!* That you'll destroy that damn video and anything else that could find its way out there to damage Jake or tarnish my memory. That you'll prevent *anyone else* from doing the same. If something gets out, Billy, whether you're directly responsible or not, it's on you. Do you understand what I'm saying?"

"Yes, yes. I do. I do. Yes!"

"Because if you break that pledge, what happens to you is *way* worse than what was behind Door Number One. And it's not just till you fucking die, Billy, it's forever. You got that?"

"Got it!"

"So which door you gonna choo—?"

"Two! Door Two! You win. But you'll leave me the fuck alone, right? No more visitations?"

"Well, it's sort of like it was when you filmed us having sex back in Cedar Rapids. I didn't know anyone would be watching me. And now, you won't know when I'm watching you. But believe me, Billy boy, I'll know if you've broken your promise. And you'll know, too. Remember, hell hath no fury like a woman scorned."

"What?"

"Learned it in English lit at Briscoe JC. Look it up, asshole."

And then, as best I can tell, she's gone.

CHAPTER FIFTY-TWO

Christie

These past few months have been an emotional rollercoaster. My dinner with Jake in San Diego was transformational, or so it seemed. Yet here I sit, in my tiny Tucson apartment, moping, pondering what might have been.

I was attracted to Jake from the moment we met—at the job interview in his office. Big, handsome guy, smart, articulate, a sense of humor. You'd be hard pressed to find a more appealing specimen. But it was the job I was after, not Jake. Between the ring on his finger and the rules of the workplace, there was nothing to contemplate.

For two years, we worked together daily. He mentored me, molded me into a capable and productive lawyer. He was patient, kind, unfailingly generous with his time and knowledge. Our working relationship ripened naturally into friendship. We cared about each other, but not in a romantic way. Had circumstances been different, our mutual affection might have evolved into something more, but we toed the line out of mutual respect.

When cracks surfaced in Jake's marriage, our mutual restraint was tested. Some women might have offered a modicum of physical comfort in addition to moral support, but I wasn't raised that way. Marriage is marriage, for better or worse, and I couldn't have lived with myself as a co-conspirator to adultery. I could tell, from the way Jake looked at me—the yearning in his eyes—that he was grappling with the same dilemma. But he, too, restrained himself. I loved him for that.

When Jake addressed the issue head-on in Flagstaff, I was relieved. He told me of his conversation with Nick, the mandate I refer to kiddingly as "Nick's Decrees of Separation." In the guise of laying down rules, we acknowledged our mutual affection and redoubled our commitment to restraint.

And then came the unimaginable: Kate's gruesome death. Jake was dumbfounded; he didn't know how to react. I could tell he'd lost his bearings, beginning with that surreal moment at the funeral when he decked Pastor Bastard. Not that the sleazy cleric didn't have it coming, but it shocked and troubled me nonetheless. I wanted so much to wrap my arms around him, tell him everything would be okay. But what could I do? Some thought I was already his mistress; the rest watched with suspicion, waiting for me to trip up so they could cluck their disapproval. So, I held myself back. I allowed myself to witness his turmoil, and did nothing to ease it. It tore at me. And over it all hung Nick's edict, like the Sword of Damocles, an acknowledgment of the romantic tinderbox that had threatened at times to ignite, and a warning of the consequences if it did. So, I held my ground, as poor Jake drifted further and further from his moorings.

As Jake lost focus, I picked up the slack in the office, shouldering the workload of two. I told myself I was doing it for him, to ease his burden. Then came the infatuation with baseball: he'd become a boy rediscovering a dream he'd thought he'd buried a decade ago. It gave him comfort, tethered him, so I forgave his neglect. But I wondered how long I could exist in this limbo.

Jake was apologetic for the extra work. Beyond that, however, he seemed curiously indifferent. Then Nick revealed Jake's obsession with the posthumous Kate, his alleged conversations with a ghost. When Jake had learned of Kate's infidelity with Pastor Bastard, he'd called *me* for comfort and advice. But now, he seeks solace in someone no longer here, instead of someone who is. And as for the rumors that he's been shacking up with a neighbor, I can't pretend not to be hurt, though I have no right to be.

The trip to San Diego was a pilgrimage of sorts. I'd hoped for signs of the old Jake, the one I'd long adored. I wanted him to see that I was still here, waiting for him, whenever he was ready. There was too much excitement and activity to discuss any of these weighty matters that first night, which is why he invited me to dinner the next.

I was nervous. I bought that stupid, racist hat as an icebreaker. We beat around the bush for a while, pretty much as I might have predicted. Then he took the bull by the horns. "How would you feel," he said, "if I leaned over this table and kissed you?" You can't imagine how my heart soared.

The stage was set. The promise of a romantic relationship was exhilarating. But I had a plane to catch. He invited me to visit him in Cleveland. Thirty major league cities and he has to play in Cleveland! But I'd have visited him anywhere. Were we prepared to ignore Nick's Decrees of Separation? He was. And I was, too. I'd waited so long for this. Jake and I worked out the dates—a weekend in late September.

But then came the news reports and the photos on social media. No, I'm not much into that, but have friends who are. Photos of Jake with a starlet on his arm. I flipped on the TV. I never watch those entertainment gossip shows, but there I was, staring in horror, as the announcer spun the rumors, displaying the photos by the paparazzi in their full glory.

"Word is that baseball heartthrob Jake Singer has been seen in L.A. in the company of actress Madelyn Moss, star of . . ." She's gorgeous: luxurious blond hair; iridescent eyes the color of blue topaz; small, pouty lips; even small, pouty hips! My breasts, maybe, are a little bit bigger, but hers are like Kate's. Jake's smiling in the photos. He's looking at her, and she's smiling right back at him, like she's ready to devour him.

I've googled Madelyn Moss on the internet. Five-foot-five. Twenty-seven years of age, already married and divorced once. No kids. Born and raised in Ohio, an Indians' fan. One year of college. Is there a brain in that pretty little skull?

To find out, I watched a YouTube interview. She gushes, she sighs, she giggles, she pouts! All the attributes of an airhead. But then I thought about Kate. Now, I'm not saying Kate was an airhead, though the choices she'd made would have made you wonder. But she wasn't Jake's intellectual equal. I'm not saying that I am, but, well . . .

Two days later, another report. On Facebook this time. "P.R. representatives for Madelyn Moss confirm her interest in Cleveland Indians' sensation Jake Singer. Singer, Moss's people claim, is equally infatuated with the young star." I'd had enough. My bubble had burst. I'd been worried about competing with a dead wife, but now I was competing with one of Hollywood's hottest young starlets? No, count me out. I was wasting my time.

I called Jake to cancel the weekend. I didn't have the courage to tell him why. I didn't mention Madelyn. Neither did he. He sounded disappointed, but I knew he'd have no trouble replacing me. He was, after all, baseball's "most eligible bachelor."

Our romance was over before it began.

CHAPTER FIFTY-THREE

Jake

The Indians were mired in third place, ten games behind the Division-leading Detroit Tigers, when I joined the club in the third week of August. Since then, we've been nearly invincible, winning twenty-four of our next thirty. Now, on Friday, September 27th, we're tied with the fading Tigers, preparing to host them in a three-game weekend set that will end the regular season, determine the division champion, and clinch a spot in the American League playoffs. Tonight, I'll start the first game before 35,000 fans—one of whom was supposed to be Christie Loring.

I looked forward to Christie's visit like a high school senior anticipating prom night. I was both nervous and pumped. But on Wednesday night, she called to cancel. She'd been overwhelmed by work, she alleged, needed the weekend to catch up. Her excuse seemed disingenuous. Felt like a punch in the gut. She'd seemed receptive, even eager, when we'd planned it in San Diego. We were poised to give it a shot. Something was amiss, but I didn't know what.

Kate's not here to console me. She's been uncharacteristically absent these past few days. While the media portrays me (falsely) as a 'chick magnet,' women—dead and alive—abandon me in droves. "Have an errand to run," Kate told me on Tuesday. The flesh-and-blood Kate would say that to camouflage a three-hour shopping spree. Do dead women shop? For three days running?

As I prepare to leave my apartment for the ballpark, I'm buoyed by the return of Kate's voice.

"Sorry, Jake. Errand took longer than expected," she says, "and I made a wrong turn."

"You had me worried. Where've you been?"

"Told you, Jake. Had an errand to run." It's not her custom to be secretive, except about Pastor Bastard and Billy Garabedian.

"Christie cancelled," I report.

"I know." She says it as if she shares my disappointment. "We'll discuss it later." Her voice is firm. "We've got a game to play."

I gather my scouting reports and catch a cab to Progressive Park. It's my final start of the regular season. Unless we win two of three, it could be my last of the year. A victory in the series opener is crucial.

By now, Silvio has resigned himself to letting me call my game—or, more accurately, letting *us* call *our* game. Loath to tinker with success, even Judd Masters is content to leave me alone.

The game is scoreless in the third when all hell breaks loose. I surrender a single to start the inning. Kate informs me of the next batter's intent to lay down a bunt. In anticipation, I charge the plate, field the bunt, and fire to second for the first out. Larry Wagner relays to first, completing the double play.

No sooner does umpiring crew chief Randy Meyer signal the runner out at first, than Tigers' manager Davey Baines catapults from the dugout. He waves frantically for time. His face is redder than Chief Wahoo's. He beckons the other umpires for a conference. Meyer asks Marty Milano to join the confab.

"What's going on, Kate?" I ask.

"Tigers' manager thinks you're talking with someone who's stealing their signs."

"Well I am, Kate."

"He thinks you're wired. Wants to check you for electronic devices."

"What the . . ."

Meyer approaches the mound. "Baines thinks you're wired up, like a stoolie. Insists I check you out," he explains. "Thinks you were too quick to field that bunt." He inspects my ears, empties my pockets, peers under my cap. A search of the mound reveals nothing discarded in haste. Moments later, as the capacity crowd mutters in confusion, Meyer escorts me off the field and into the umpires' dressing room. "Been umpiring thirty years." He laughs. "This is a first." Five minutes later, I stand in my underwear, as the crew chief pats me down like a prison guard.

"Good thing you didn't wear those polka-dotted boxers I gave you last Christmas," quips Kate. I smile, hoping Meyer won't misconstrue it as enjoying the pat down.

"Who the hell are you talking to out there?" asks the crew chief, after confirming the absence of electronics.

I answer him directly. "My dead wife. Can you cite me anything in the rule book that prohibits that?"

"I can't, counselor," says the crew chief. "You can talk to her all night as far as I'm concerned. I'm sorry about this—and the loss of your wife—but I had no choice."

"Forget it, Randy."

We return to the field where the umpires publicly

exonerate me. Baines is livid. "Dead wife, my ass!" he thunders, loud enough for the TV field mikes to pick up.

"You know this'll be all over the news and the papers," Kate says.

"Common knowledge already, Kate. Nobody's gonna be foolish enough to believe you actually exist."

"You do, don't you, lover?"

All I could do was roll my eyes.

The season's most bizarre interruption notwithstanding, Kate and I dispatch the Tigers' lineup with our customary efficiency en route to a 3-1 victory and a one-game lead in the division. We're almost there.

CHAPTER FIFTY-FOUR

Jake

The post-game press briefing is a zoo. Bloated by the presence of members of the national sports press, the media room is standing room only.

"They're gonna be all over you, trying to twist your words, make you sound like an idiot," Marty whispers, as we sit down at the podium before the throng of reporters. "Keep it simple," he counsels. "Don't give 'em anything they can hang you on." He turns to the reporters. "Okay, first question."

The inquisition begins in earnest. "Jake, can you tell us what took place in the umpire's dressing room in the third inning?"

"Randy and I played a couple hands of strip poker. I lost." Laughter all around.

"How badly?" someone yells out.

"Badly enough for an "R" rating." More laughter.

"What do you think he was looking for?" The question comes from the back of the room.

"The Lost Ark?" I suggest.

"Were you wearing electronic devices of any kind, Jake?"

I respond like a lawyer. "I was wearing a regulation uniform and the undergarments appropriate thereto."

Then came the question I'd been expecting. "Davey Baines thought you were having a conversation with someone out there on the mound. Were you talking to someone, Jake?"

"I suppose that depends upon your definition of *someone*."

"Do you converse with your late wife out there, Jake?" asks a member of the national media. Marty looks at me. His eyes are telling me to restrain myself, for my own good.

"That's a metaphysical conundrum. I certainly talk to myself," I say, preparing to ramp up to total obfuscation. "A conversation presupposes a second participant, and to suggest there's another participant is to make assumptions that would require a panel of philosophers or paranormal experts to evaluate. I'm not qualified in either discipline." Blank looks everywhere.

"Metaphysical conundrum? Can you rephrase that, Jake?"

"Probably, but it wouldn't provide the answer I think you're hoping to hear."

"So, are you saying you *don't* talk to your wife?"

"Asked and answered!" Marty interjects, a giant smile on his face. "I watch the courtroom dramas, gentlemen." His snappy response puts an effective halt to that line of questioning. The rest of the session is anticlimactic.

The Indians clinch the Central Division title the following evening, drubbing a disconsolate Tigers' ballclub by a 12-2 score. Under the byzantine rules that govern Major League Baseball's post-season, the Indians are now obliged to capture a best-of-five-game Division Series against the Western Division champion Los Angeles Angels. If we prevail, we take on the winner of another divisional matchup pitting the Eastern Division champion, Boston Red Sox, against this year's "wild card" qualifier, the very same Detroit Tigers we've just defeated. The winner of a best-of-seven series between the two playoff winners moves on to the World Series. I explain it all to Kate.

"Phew!" Kate gasps. "Now, let me see if I've got this straight. We just won the Central Division by beating the Tigers, right?"

"Right."

"But, if we beat the Angels and the Tigers beat the Red Sox, then we have to beat the Tigers all over again?"

"That's right."

"But we just beat the Tigers."

"Right."

"So, they get a second chance?"

"I guess you could say that."

"But if we lose to the Angels, do we get a second chance?"

"No."

"Who's on first?" she asks, channeling Lou Costello.

We open the Division Series at home. I arrive at the clubhouse early. Though I don't start until Game Two, I begin poring over the scouting reports on the Angels' hitters. Marty pops his head out of his office and waves me inside. Sitting there is Brendan Baker, the young, hard-hitting first baseman I played with at Columbus.

"I think you two know each other," Marty says. Travis Bates tweaked his balky hamstring in the Detroit series, so the Indians activated Brendan to replace him. "Brendan tells me that in addition to your pitching and media skills, you've got a knack for predicting what an opposing pitcher's gonna throw."

I'd hoped that Kate and I wouldn't be asked to reprise that performance. "Well, I—"

"One-for-one with a game- and steak-winning homer," Brendan boasts.

"Anything to this, Jake?"

I suddenly face a dilemma. So far as I know, Kate's not in the room. She could be anywhere. Will she turn up for tonight's game? If she does, is she willing to lend her skills to buck up the Indians' offense?

"I've only tried it once," I tell Marty. "Probably just dumb luck."

"We need all the luck we can get," Marty says, "dumb or otherwise." He scratches his hairless head thoughtfully. "Okay, then. I leave it to the two of you to work out."

CHAPTER FIFTY-FIVE

Kate

"You here, Kate?" Jake is alone in the weight room off the clubhouse.

"Um hmm," I mutter.

"You okay?"

"Got a sore knee," I say, "and my back is killing me."

"Funny."

"Actually, Jake, I'm tired. Not sure what it is, but I don't have that bounce in my step anymore."

"Joking again?"

"Not entirely," I admit. "Need something, lover?"

Jake tells me about his meeting with Brendan and Marty. "Will you do it, Kate?"

"Well, yeah . . . I guess so." What choice do I have?

Brendan bats ninth, so I don't have to drag myself to the mound until the third inning. As the Angels' pitcher receives the sign from his catcher, I report the pitch selection, which Jake relays to Brendan from the steps of the dugout. It's not as if I actually decode the sign—I simply absorb the pitcher's interpretation of the catcher's signal. On the third pitch, Brendan drives a ball hard to right field, but it's hauled in for an easy out.

He hits it on the nose again in the fifth, but again to no avail.

With the score tied, Brendan bats again in the seventh. A single, but the Indians leave him stranded.

Bottom of the ninth now, tied at two, with the winning run on second. Perfect opportunity, but Brendan fans. He's losing confidence in Jake's pitch-divining skills. "Doesn't take a genius to anticipate a fastball from a guy who throws nothing but heat," he tells Jake, shaking his head as he returns to the dugout.

"Doesn't take a genius to hit it, either," I vent to Jake.

The game goes on... and on. In the bottom of the thirteenth, Zack Holt, the Angels' flame-throwing reliever, is on the mound. After striking out the first two Indians' batters, he endures a patch of wildness, walking three in a row. Brendan's up with the bases loaded.

Jake relays to Brendan the pitch I glean from the mind of Holt: a fastball on the outside corner. I turn my attention to Brendan. His mind's a cinch to read—nitwits are always the easiest. "Okay," he's thinking, "if the fuckin' ball's coming in on the outside corner, I'll just cheat a little, lean into the pitch, and take it to the opposite field." Might have been a good plan if the pitcher had command of his fastball, but Brendan forgets that Holt can't find the plate. As the Angels' righty winds up and throws, Brendan dives over the plate, ready to pounce on that outside fastball. Holt badly misses his target, but hits another.

"Ooooooouch!" shrieks Baker, as the hurler's misfire bears in on him, slamming into his right ass cheek with the force of a bazooka round. The crowd lets out a brief gasp, then a loud cheer. While Brendan winces in pain, his teammates leap from the dugout in elation, prodding him to stagger to first while the runner on third skips home with the winning run.

"Not the way we planned it," I say to Jake, as he sprints from the dugout and onto the field to join in the celebration.

CHAPTER FIFTY-SIX

Jake

Everyone's exhausted after our marathon opening-game victory. Even Kate seems drained. While I'm chomping at the bit, hyped for my first post-season start, Kate offers scant encouragement.

"What's up, Kate?" I ask.

She yawns. I'd never heard Kate do that before—posthumously, that is.

"Late night?"

"Fuck, yeah. Thirteen innings, Jake," she grouses. "For some reason, I just don't have the same spunk I had in my younger days."

"You're dead, Kate," I remind her. "Are you ready for tonight's start?"

"Sure, Jake," she says, without enthusiasm.

Kate's lethargy is obvious as we plow through the first two innings. I find myself deferring to Silvio's calls with favorable results.

In the third inning, Kate is AWOL. I circle the mound, fiddle with the rosin bag, hoping to hear her voice. "Where are you, Kate?" I mutter under my breath. No response. I walk the leadoff man, always a bad sign.

With the second batter of the inning at the plate, I go into my stretch, check the runner on first, and begin my motion. In the midst of my delivery, Kate announces her presence. "He's primed for your fastball!" she yells, just as I'm about to throw one. Her tardy warning knocks me off stride. My right foot slips and I land awkwardly, crumbling to the ground. The pitch bounces ten feet short of the plate. A hush comes over the crowd as I grab my ankle. While Silvio chases the errant pitch, the runner advances to second. Silvio calls time-out.

Marty, Judd, and Rudy, our trainer, sprint from the dugout.

"You okay, lover?" asks Kate, sheepishly.

"No, goddammit!"

Silvio reaches me first. "Who the fook you talking at, rook?" he asks.

"Never mind," I grunt. "Help me up!"

But Rudy insists I stay put. He bends down to check my ankle, manipulating it as if he were molding clay. "Does this hurt?" he asks. "How about this?"

"Yes, dammit," I screech. As I do, Marty raises his right arm, signaling the bullpen for a reliever. Judd and Rudy lift me up and help me off the field.

Kate is contrite as I lie on a training room table. "I'm so sorry, Jake," she says, "I haven't been myself lately." I can't respond, as Rudy and his assistant are attending to me. A few minutes later, I'm wheeled out for an X-ray. The results come swiftly.

"Nothing broken," Rudy says. "Looks like a grade-one ankle sprain."

"What does that mean?"

"You'll need to stay off it for a few days," he says.

"How long before I pitch again?"

"Depends upon how you respond to treatment." I push Rudy for something more precise. "At least a couple of weeks, more likely three," he tells me. "You're thirty-three, Jake, not twenty."

"Shit!" Three weeks knocks me out of the Division Series and the League Championship Series, assuming we get there. If we make the World Series, I'm questionable, at best.

Rudy elevates the ankle, applies ice packs, and leaves me alone in the trainer's room to stew. I spit out a few choice expletives, huff a few times, and apologize to my dead wife.

"That's okay," Kate says. "I deserve it. I don't know what's wrong with me."

"Where were you at the start of the inning, Kate?"

"You won't believe me if I tell you," she says.

"Try me."

"Angels' locker room." I hear what sounds like a deep sigh. "I can't do anything right on the first try anymore," she laments. I think she wants to say something more, but clams up instead. I'm frightened of losing her.

Over the next three weeks, I spend every waking hour in the training room, in a desperate quest to return to the mound before the end of our post-season run. My teammates keep extending the deadline. After winning the Division Series in four games, we capture the Championship Series in six. The World Series opens the day after tomorrow against the National League champion Chicago Cubs at Progressive Field in Cleveland.

I'm on a training table with ice on my shoulder and a stim machine hooked to my ankle when Marty walks in with Clay Burton, our wunderkind general manager. Just a couple years older than I, he looks like a pimple-faced teenager.

"How you feeling, Jake?" Clay asks. It's a loaded question.

"Never better," I lie.

"Tell 'im the truth, Jake," Marty orders. "We've got twenty-four hours before we set our Series roster, and I don't want you wasting a slot if you can't make it back."

I hold nothing back. "I'm jogging without any pain," I tell them. "Throwing at three-quarters intensity from flat ground with no ill effects."

Marty looks at Clay. "Rudy's gonna put him through a battery of tests in the morning," he tells Clay. "Thinks he'll be able to give us some innings out of the pen toward the latter part of the Series." Marty turns to me. "But you're gonna need to really push to get there."

"I'd love to have your arm in our arsenal, Jake, even if it's only out of the pen," Clay says.

I vow to do whatever it takes.

"Okay, then. Let's see how those drills go in the morning," Clay says, "and how your arm feels after throwing from the mound. We'll make the final call then, all right?"

"I'll be ready," I say. "Promise."

CHAPTER FIFTY-SEVEN

Kate

Six months have passed since that big rig flattened my fanny. Still, I linger in the land of the living. I miss my physical self, that nimble and sensuous body that Jake so admired, the body that Billy and the Pastor so shamefully exploited. But I can still think and communicate. And my capacity for love is undiminished. I love my widowed husband dearly. And while I haven't unraveled the mystery of my continuing existence, I've given it a purpose: to restore the happiness I stole from Jake during those last troubled months of our marriage.

So, what have I accomplished in six months of death? More than your average stiff, perhaps, but not nearly enough.

Jake loved baseball before he loved me, and it was cruelly ripped from his grasp. With a little encouragement—and some ghostly advice—his Little League dreams have come true. I've cherished every moment of our collaboration on the ball field. It's brought me closer to Jake than I'd ever been in life. And, while I'd like to think that my pitch-calling skills made a difference, that wouldn't be fair to Jake. My presence gave him confidence—made him feel invincible on that mound—but it was Jake's fastball that mowed down batters, his crazy curve that tied them in knots, his changeup that threw them off stride. On the occasions he was on his own, he was just as effective. I'm glad I nudged him along, but he deserves all of the credit for what he's accomplished.

And then there's my haunting of Billy Garabedian. I haven't disclosed that to Jake. He doesn't need to know. Until then, I'd revealed myself only to Jake. I don't count that tattoo-laden biker I spooked in the park on the day of my resurrection—that was just practice. Intimidating Billy required communication, so I spoke to him, cowing him into submission like he'd once done to me. I'm sure now he'll toe the line: Jake will be safe, as well as my memory. And revenge, though not my primary objective, was a delightfully unexpected bonus. Frightening him into wetting his shorts was precious. To die for, you might say.

But my work isn't finished. There's one last thing to accomplish—the most important of all—the restoration of Jake's love life. He needs someone alive in every sense of the word, someone better suited to him than I was, who can make him happier than I could. Trouble is, left to his own devices, Jake doesn't always choose wisely. He picked me, for instance. Then it was Big Red, a carrot-colored recipe for disaster. He was even tempted, however briefly, by a slinky actress who milked him for his public relations value.

I've no time to waste. I sense my days are numbered, that my powers are fading. Piercing batters' minds is more wearying, teleportation more treacherous. I can't fail Jake. Not again. There's no time for subtlety and discretion. I revealed myself to Billy out of a sense of urgency. Now, it's time to call on Christie.

CHAPTER FIFTY-EIGHT

Jake

At eight in the morning, Rudy accompanies me onto the field. There's an autumn chill in the air. Marty, Judd, and Clay huddle near the dugout steps. Under their watchful eyes, Rudy runs me through a battery of drills. My ankle holds up. The brain trust nods in approval.

Judd directs me to the mound as Silvio emerges from the dugout. He wears shin guards and a chest protector over a garish warm-up suit. "Leet's go, rook!" he barks.

I stride to the mound, trying to look nonchalant. I feel like I'm taking a college entrance exam. Pass and you're in the World Series; flunk and your dreams are shattered. I won't admit to the tenderness lingering in my right ankle. It's normal, I convince myself. I can do this.

Judd flips me a ball. I roll it around in my fingers, assume a fastball grip, and squeeze the baseball into my glove. I wind up and throw. *Thwack!* "Atta boy, Jake!" Silvio cries out. "Again!" I throw it again, a little harder.

"Lemme see Uncle Charlie!" Silvio bleats. That's slang for a curveball. I shove the ball against the stump of my finger and deliver a sharp-breaking curve. "Muy bueno!" cries Silvio.

After thirty pitches, Judd shuts me down. Marty jogs to the mound for the post-mortem.

"How do you feel?" Marty asks.

"Great," I say. He gives me a look. "Okay, so there's just a hint of tenderness, but I can pitch through it, no problem."

"Judd? Silvio?"

"He looks fine to me," Judd tells Marty. Silvio concurs.

Clay, who's been talking with Rudy, joins the conversation. "Whaddya think, Marty?" he asks.

"I need him, Clay. I'll hold 'im back till later in the Series if I can, but I'd love to have his arm out of the pen," Marty says. "Cubbies haven't seen him before. He's kind of a secret weapon."

"Okay, Jake, welcome to the World Series," Clay says. My heart turns somersaults in my chest.

CHAPTER FIFTY-NINE

Kate

I used to fear Christie Loring. She's beautiful, smart, and unattached. The more I botched my marriage, the more she worried me. Yet, even as I drove a wedge between us with my endless cavalcade of blunders, Jake remained faithful, and Christie endured like a nun. For that, she's earned my grudging respect. But is Christie the cure for Jake's snake-bitten love life?

Jake would kill me—if it weren't redundant—if he'd known I'd been eavesdropping in San Diego at his dinner with Christie. He'd laid the groundwork for a romantic relationship. She was ecstatic. Outwardly, she played it cool, like I did on the day I met Jake at the Harvard Square Pub. He invited her to spend a weekend in Cleveland. At first, she pooh-poohed the idea. Then she accepted, before wriggling out at the last minute. I have to know why.

After an alarming number of telepathic miscalculations, I find myself in Christie's apartment, awaiting her arrival. It's nine when she walks in the door. She's fried from another long day at the office.

Hungry and thirsty, she opens the refrigerator, staring blankly at its contents. There's less there than I'd left Jake before my ill-fated trip to the Rincon Market. She pulls out some leftover chicken, shoves it into the microwave, and taps the controls. She prepares herself a side salad: cherry tomatoes, some sad-looking arugula, a dash of bottled dressing. When the microwave beeps, she removes the chicken, grabs some cutlery, pours herself some wine. She slumps to the table and eats in a stupor.

I tap into her thoughts, gingerly at first, feeling like the intruder I am. But I persist—after all, this is partly a reconnaissance mission. She thinks about the office, the long list of matters she hasn't addressed. Then, in a moment of weakness, she thinks about Jake, about that bony starlet Madelyn Moss, about her fading prospects for happiness. *What's the use?* she asks herself. She gulps down the wine. *I made the right call,* she tells herself, without commitment. *He's got himself a starlet, what would he want with me?*

As I assemble the bits and pieces floating through Christie's mind, I understand exactly what's happened. Intimidated by the news reports and social media gossip about Jake and Madelyn Moss, she's assumed the worst. That's why she cancelled her weekend with Jake.

"You've got it all wrong!" I blurt out, no longer able to restrain myself. It's an awkward introduction, particularly for a ghost.

Christie leaps from her chair, nearly choking on a forkful of wilted arugula. Her heart's pounding. "Who's there!" she cries out in terror.

"It's okay, Christie," I say. "Don't be frightened." What makes me think that soothing words from a ghost will have a calming effect on the living? Christie remains on her feet, glancing into every corner of the apartment.

"You're not crazy, and there's no one here," I assure her, however lamely.

"That proves just the opposite!" she screams. "Who . . . *where* the hell are—"

"Please, Christie, stay calm," I beg her. "In fact, you might want to pour yourself another glass of wine." Dumb.

Christie hesitates. She considers pouring herself that wine, but thinks better of it. She begins to shiver. I forget how scary I must be. Death is a *formidable* social disability, as Jake might say.

"I really didn't mean to scare you. I'm really sorry."

She sits, her face ashen. "Tell me who and where you are and why you're here. Please!"

"It's Kate Singer."

"What?" Poor girl looks like she's seen a ghost. Of course, as we all know by now, she's only heard one.

"You heard correctly," I say. "You can't see me. I just wanna talk with you." This seems more and more like a bad idea. Is my meddling sabotaging my mission? Am I the world's most incompetent ghost?

"Look, *Kate*, or whomever you are. I don't know how you're doing this, but I'd prefer you leave. Please!" Polite, even as her fear turns to anger. I'm impressed.

"Let's start over," I suggest. "First, let me explain a few things." I tell her about my death, my funeral, my 'existence,' and my ability to comprehend her thoughts. Her fear evolves into astonishment. "You've been thinking about Jake and that damn movie actress," I tell her, "and you're second-guessing your decision to cancel that weekend with Jake."

"How can you possibly—"

"I told you, I can read your mind."

"Okay," she says, "assuming for a moment you are who you say you are, and I'm not completely bonkers, why are you here?"

Now, we're getting somewhere. "Because you're mistaken

about Jake. You're crazy about him, and he feels the same way about you."

"Then why's he posing with Madelyn Moss with that big smile on his face."

"He was suckered into a P.R. trap. Madelyn Moss is nothing to Jake. She met him once, at her agent's invitation, got her photos, and moved on," I say, recounting what Jake had explained to me weeks ago.

"Why do you care about Jake and me? I thought you despised me."

"I was jealous of you, Christie. But I knew in my heart Jake was faithful. I haven't stopped loving him. I want him to be happy."

"Where *are* you?" she asks again, wondering where to direct her gaze.

"Listen, Christie, it's not too late. You can fly out to the Series."

"I've got way too much work," she protests.

"Then fly to Chicago for the weekend, for the middle three games of the Series. I'll get him to leave you some tickets. He'll be ecstatic," I assure her. "There's nothing to keep you from each other now. Not even me. And screw Nick's rules. You two were meant for each other. *Please*, Christie. Please do this . . . for both of you . . . and for me."

"I need to get my head around this," she says, with a long sigh. "I'll . . . I'll think about it." She rubs her temples vigorously. "Jesus," she mutters, "this is insane! I'm really, truly, talking to . . . someone . . . who's—"

"Dead. Yes, I'm afraid so. But for your own good, don't admit it to anyone, except maybe Jake. Later on, that is. Because," I continue, "if he knew I was here, he'd kill me!"

"But you're already—"

"Figure of speech."

CHAPTER SIXTY

Jake

"Where have you been?" I ask, after Kate reveals her presence in my apartment late Monday morning, the day before the Series opens. "You've been missing for days."

"Another errand," Kate says.

"These disappearances are becoming more frequent. Is everything all right?"

"I'm still dead, if that's what you mean."

"Okay, fine." I tell her I made the roster; she emits a slightly muffled squeal of joy. "They'll probably hold me out until later in the Series," I add, "to give the ankle more time to heal."

"I'm happy for you, lover," she says. "Listen, why don't you invite Nick, Trudy, and Christie to come up for the games?"

"Nick promised to come to Cleveland for the last two games, assuming we play them. I probably won't pitch before then anyway."

"How about Christie?"

"Don't know what to think," I tell Kate. "Either she got cold feet, or I completely misread her in San Diego. Tried to call her several times, but she won't return my calls."

"Still, it can't hurt to ask, right?" I'm intrigued by her growing interest in Christie.

No, it can't hurt to ask. I call her at the office, but get her voicemail. I leave a message, inviting her to any or all of the games. I tell her where the team will be staying in Chicago. "I'll leave you tickets at the Will Call windows at both ballparks. Come if you can," I say, trying not to sound desperate.

Christie doesn't call back, and she doesn't show up for the first two games in Cleveland, which the two clubs split, as I bide my time in the bullpen.

It's Friday night, third game of the World Series and the first at Chicago's Wrigley Field. Cool, early autumn gusts swirl in from Lake Michigan. My eyes are drawn to the antiquated scoreboard, an expanse of forest-green rising majestically over the center field bleachers. The ivy-covered walls enthrall me. I pinch myself, humbled by my very presence in this hallowed place.

The game is tight, the lead changing hands repeatedly as the night progresses. We trail by a run in the top of the ninth when Silvio slams a three-run homer. Our closer's on for the bottom of the ninth, but Judd calls down to the pen to start me warming. It's mostly an excess of caution, I figure, and a chance to limber up for later in the Series.

Our closer tames the Cubs, and we win Game Three. I change, shower, and return to my hotel room. It's after midnight. I summon Kate, but get no answer. Minutes later, there's a knock on my door. Kate never knocks—couldn't if she wanted to.

It's Christie. For the second time in a week, my heart nearly leaps from my chest. She's wearing that stupid Chief Wahoo hat and a sheepish grin. I bend down, lift the hat off her head, and, with some trepidation, plant a kiss on her forehead. She drops her bag and wraps her arms around me. We kiss like Bogart and Bergman in *Casablanca*.

"Why didn't you call me?" I finally ask her.

She mentions Madelyn Moss.

"You're better looking," I assure her, "and you've got both a heart and a brain." She doesn't explain what allayed her concerns about the actress. I suspect Kate's involvement, but I'm not going to risk asking Christie if my dead wife has paid her a visit.

I take Christie's bag, pour her a drink from the minibar, and we talk. But not for long. We both have the same agenda: one too long deferred. I take her hand, we retire to the bed, and pursue that agenda for the rest of the evening, breaking every rule in Nick's book.

CHAPTER SIXTY-ONE

Jake

I awaken on Saturday morning with a smile on my face and Christie by my side.

"The earth moved," she says, sweetly.

"Fracking," I deadpan.

Christie stays for the weekend, catching an early morning flight to Tucson on Monday. Kate's still a no-show, and while I'm grateful for the privacy, I can't keep from worrying.

We split the last two games in Chicago, and fly back to Cleveland, up three games to two. Nick calls late Monday evening to let me know he's in town, and I finagle him a clubhouse pass for Game Six the next day.

"Would have never believed this possible," Nick says, wowed by the glamour and commotion of the clubhouse. "And all because I circled a tryout announcement in the *Daily Star*."

"A lot's happened since then, Nick," I remind him.

"Speaking of which," he says, "Christie didn't make it into the office yesterday until late afternoon. Said she had to visit a sick aunt." He chuckles. "That's bullshit, right?"

"What, aunts don't get sick?"

"Never mind," he says.

I have to cut the reunion short for yet another round of

training room torture. I'm like a car on a lift, attended by a team of overzealous mechanics.

"How they treatin' ya, Jake?" Emerging from my body makeover in the training room, I'm confronted by the sight and voice of Harley McGinnis.

"Great to see you, Harley," I say. I tease him by telling him my father's in town for the rest of the Series. "I suppose you'd like to pay your respects."

Harley grins. "Guess your Dad neglected to tell you," he says. "He buttonholed me in the stands at Wrigley. Thought he was fixing to blast me again, but he walks up and shakes my hand. 'Better late than never,' he says, and thanks me for being a 'persistent old fuck.'"

"Sounds like Dad."

"Hope to see ya on the mound before this is over," Harley says. He gives me a bear hug, wishes me luck, dispenses a hearty guffaw, and ambles off.

It's approaching game time, so I finish dressing, head through the dugout and out to the bullpen. When no one's listening, I call out Kate's name, but get no reply.

CHAPTER SIXTY-TWO

Kate

I've lost time, somehow. I misfired after visiting Christie. I set my sights on Cleveland, focused like a laser, but nothing happened. So here I am, still mired in Christie's apartment when she returns from the office with her overnight bag on Monday evening.

"Hey," I say as she walks in. My greeting startles her. She drops her bag on her foot and yelps in pain.

"Kate?"

"Anyone else haunting this place?"

"I don't understand. Why are you here again?"

"I never left," I tell her. "I'm experiencing what you might call technical difficulties."

I can hear her thinking. *What does she mean by 'technical difficulties'? Do I ask if she's okay? What would I do if she wasn't? Do I just go on bantering with Jake's dead wife as if it were normal?* And the reliable old standard, *am I crazy?*

"I can 'hear' you, Christie," I remind her. "And no, there's nothing you can do, other than tell me how your weekend went with Jake . . . oh, and how the Indians did."

Christie's humongous smile tells me all I need to know about her time with Jake, and she fills me in on the status of the Series. I'm pleased on both counts. I'm relieved to learn that Jake hasn't pitched yet. I'd be devastated if he thought I'd abandoned him. The Cubs victory in Game Five means that the Series returns to Cleveland. If I can only find my way out of Tucson!

"Is there anything I can do for you?" Christie asks.

Surprisingly, there is. "Help me get back to Cleveland." I say nothing about joining Jake on the mound.

"How can I do that?" she asks, continuing to assess her sanity.

"There's precedent," I say, dazzling her with my knowledge of legalese. "I hitched a ride with Jake from Allentown to San Diego. I stayed close, joined him on the plane, cabbed from the airport. It worked then, so maybe it'll work now." Christie wasn't planning on flying to Cleveland tomorrow—she'd just returned from Chicago—but maybe I can guilt her into changing her plans.

"Uh . . . I wasn't—"

"I know, but I think you should. For a lot of reasons," I say. "Listen, the next day or two could be the most important in Jake's life. You need to be there. You'll share his joy if they win, ease his pain if they lose. Either way, it'll mean the world to him . . . and to you, too."

Christie's head is spinning. She's thinking about her clients, her obligations. Nick, she knows, is already in Cleveland. Work didn't stop him. "Fuck it," she says. She picks up her phone, dials the office, and leaves a message with her secretary. "My aunt took a turn for the worse," she says. "I won't be back until Thursday . . . at the earliest."

CHAPTER SIXTY-THREE

Jake

The Cubs thump us on Tuesday night, forcing a deciding seventh game. The news is not all bad, though, as Christie makes a surprise appearance. Kate's back, too—I can feel it—but she won't acknowledge her presence. I suspect a connection with Christie, but I'm not inclined to inquire.

Through six games, I've yet to see action, but on Wednesday, Marty pulls me aside. "You're likely first out of the pen tonight," he says, "especially if there's trouble early." I assure him I'll be ready.

Mom and Dad are here, along with Nick and Christie. Assuming that Kate's here somewhere, we could stage a funeral reunion. Nick asks Christie about her sick aunt before surrendering to a fit of laughter.

Connor Davies, our starting pitcher, has been a workhorse, but his innings are taking their toll. Everyone can see that he's running on fumes. After a rough first inning, he's pounded again in the second. The bullpen phone rings. "Singer, you're up," barks the bullpen coach. I stretch and begin warming up.

As Davies continues to falter, I rush my routine. Judd visits the mound to buy me a little more time. Two batters later and Davies is toast. Marty waves me in from the pen. As I nervously jog to the mound, I summon Kate.

"Here for you, honey," she says, and I break into a smile. The butterflies disperse.

Davies has dug me a hole. In fact, it's more like a canyon. We're down 4-0, with no outs and runners on the corners. As I lean in for Silvio's first sign, Kate sounds an alarm.

"Go with Silvio," she pleads. "There's too much static . . . I can't trust my readings." In previous outings, Kate's withdrawal would leave me panicking. But I'm as confident tonight as I've been all season. I settle for her emotional support—together with Christie's.

I whiff my first batter on three pitches: a pair of 95-mile-per-hour heaters and a curve that bends like a palm tree in a hurricane. My next pitch induces an inning-ending double play. Four pitches, three outs. Kate congratulates me, transitioning seamlessly from pitch-caller to cheerleader.

I hurl a flawless third and strand a runner on second in the fourth. In our half of the fourth, Murphy rifles a two-run shot over the left field fence to cut the lead in half.

Marty pulls me over as I step into the dugout after a perfect fifth inning. "How much gas you got left in that tank, Jake?" he asks. "Can you give me another inning?"

"I can give you an entire night," I tell him.

We score again in the sixth, reducing our deficit to a single run. As we continue to bat, Judd and Marty debate the wisdom of keeping me in the game. I've thrown five shutout innings, allowing three hits. I decide to join the debate, marching to the end of the dugout where they ponder my fate. "I'm fucking fine," I say, leaving no room for doubt. "Don't even fucking *think* about pulling me!" Marty, I know, eats it up; Judd, not so much. When the inning ends, I vault from the dugout to the field before anyone can change his mind.

I feel stronger as the game progresses. My fastball's

touching 95, and my curve is devastating. Kate screams encouragement as I mow down the Cubs in order in the seventh and eighth.

Time's running out and we're still down a run.

Larry Wagner doubles to lead off the bottom of the eighth. Murphy walks. As the Cubs' manager strolls to the mound to consult his pitcher, Judd approaches me on the bench.

I spring from my perch like a jack-in-the box. "*Get the fuck away from me!*" I holler, waving him off like a madman.

"You tell heem, rook!" Silvio pipes up. Masters shakes his head, pivots, and retreats.

The Cubs make a pitching change. They bring in their closer, Manny Gomez, a burly Cuban who can throw a hundred-mile-an-hour fastball in his sleep. Typically a ninth-inning guy, he's tasked with stranding two baserunners while recording the six outs that separate the Cubs from a World Series title.

Second baseman Bobby Nelson is the first to face Gomez. I watch our third-base coach relay the signs Marty flashes from the corner of the dugout. The whole world anticipates a sacrifice bunt. As the corner infielders creep in, Nelson squares and lays the bunt down. In a single motion, the Cubs' third baseman grabs it cleanly with his bare hand and guns it to first for the out. The runners move up. Nelson collects high-fives as he descends the dugout steps. Two runners stand in scoring position with one out.

Travis Bates swaggers to the plate. It's power versus power. Gomez throws him a fastball that registers 101 on the scoreboard radar gun. "Strike one!" barks the home plate umpire. Bates is unfazed. He points his bat toward the centerfield fence like a latter-day Babe Ruth. Gomez responds with more triple-digit heat. "Strike two!" bellows the ump. As the crowd groans, Manny finishes him off with a wipeout slider.

Two out, two on, and it's Silvio's turn. He twirls his bat like a drum major as he digs into the batter's box. "Vamanos!" our Latin players cry out: *let's go!* He takes a strike . . . and then another, right down the heart of the plate, without so much as raising the bat from his shoulder. Silvio sneers while the crowd moans.

Gomez is a strike away from ending the eighth with a one-run lead. He winds and deals his best heater of the night. Silvio flicks his bat like a drumstick, lifting a soft floater to the left side. Forty thousand fans inhale in unison. The shortstop pivots, sprinting into the outfield grass. The left fielder races in. As the shortstop leaps, the ball ticks off the edge of his outstretched glove, dropping at the feet of the charging left fielder. Both runs score, giving Cleveland a one-run lead. Silvio stands at first, his fists raised triumphantly toward the heavens.

Gomez whiffs the next batter, but the damage is done. The Indians are now three outs from a World Series victory.

Our closer is ready in the bullpen. He's had an inconsistent series, so Marty's hesitant to bring him in. Judd and Marty argue vehemently, but it's Marty's call.

To the astonishment of virtually everyone, I amble to the mound for the ninth inning. Marty's taking an enormous chance, one for which he'll be second-guessed eternally if his judgment proves faulty. But the crowd loves it, cheering wildly as I run through my warm-ups.

"You can fookin' *do it!*" yells Silvio at the top of his lungs.

"You can fookin' *do it!*" mimics Kate. The chuckle she triggers loosens me up.

I retire the first two Cubs' hitters on easy groundouts.

"Just one to go, lover," Kate purrs.

The throng is on its feet. But I run into trouble. Willie Romero, the Cubs' fleet-footed centerfielder, draws a walk on a three-and-two pitch that appeared to me to nick the corner. Forty thousand umpires in the crowd confirm my judgment. But the plate umpire sees it differently. Silvio springs from his haunches, launching an epithet-laden protest, but to no avail.

Marty rises to the top step of the dugout. His body language tells me there's no leeway. Bailey Mason, the Cubs' number-two hitter, is up next. I lob to first to hold the runner. On my first pitch to Mason, Romero sprints toward second. Silvio throws to Wagner, who applies the tag for what appears to be the third out! But no! The umpire extends his arms and cries "Safe!"

"No fucking way!" screams Kate. Wagner jumps up and down in disbelief. Marty pops out to argue, but makes no headway. Two calls that, had either gone our way, would have ended the Series.

Marty makes a detour to the mound. I figure my night is over. But he doesn't reach for the baseball. Silvio joins us. Marty asks if I want to intentionally walk Mason. "No," I tell Marty. "I've got him."

Kate's voice suddenly fills my head. "He's looking dead red!" she screeches. "Don't throw him anything hard!"

Silvio proposes that I set up Mason with a couple of fastballs, then pull the string with my change-up. Marty nods his assent.

Again, Kate objects. "No fucking fastballs!" she shrieks. She's turned up the volume to the max, and my head's ringing. I can't hear myself think. I decide to say nothing, and wait until Marty returns to the dugout and Silvio to the plate.

Silvio crouches and calls for the fastball. I shake him off.

Miffed, he repeats the signal. Again, I shake him off.

"Time!" he calls, and bolts to the mound.

"What the fook?" he barks, predictably.

"I changed my mind," I tell him. Silvio glances toward the dugout in exasperation, but Marty just shrugs.

"You're one fookin' pain in the ass!" he tells me for the hundredth time, shaking his head in frustration. Finally, he turns away. "Your fookin' funeral," he mutters.

"Damn, I'm sick of hearing him say that!" Kate complains again.

Silvio calls for the curve. I unleash a beauty. Mason misses it by a foot.

On the next pitch, he signals fastball again. Again, I shake him off. He signals curve. I shake him off. "What the fook!" he shrieks, dropping three fingers to indicate change-up. Conventional wisdom says you set up your change-up with your fastball, not your curve. But our collaboration is hardly conventional. I throw the change-up. Mason is way ahead. Strike two.

Now, Silvio figures, I'll finish him off with the fastball. Wrong again! I shake him off until he orders the curve. Mason swings like he's doing the hokey-pokey, missing by a mile. Game over. Series over. *Indians win!*

Silvio flips off his mask and darts to the mound, diving into my embrace. Graham and Wagner throw their gloves into the air and join the scrum. Marty leads the charge from the dugout. Relievers stream out the bullpen gate and race toward the mound. It's pandemonium. Full-grown men are jumping up and down like four-year-olds.

A strange sensation tempers my ecstasy. I listen for Kate, but I can't hear her over the roar of the crowd and my teammates. Where is she? I break free of the scrum, and head for the section beside the dugout where my parents stand clapping and smiling. I watch in amusement as Harley McGinniss squeezes my father in a smothering bear hug. Nick is there, too, as elated as I am. Finally, I spot Christie. She's cheering wildly, her dumb Chief Wahoo hat still perched on her head. I long to kiss and hug her, but I hold myself back. The embrace of a beautiful colleague by a recent widower is still largely frowned upon, especially in Middle America. We settle for mutual smiles.

I listen in vain for a message from Kate. A television analyst drags me away for an interview. The celebration is about to begin.

CHAPTER SIXTY-FOUR

Kate

I cry out to Jake like a madwoman, but I can't get into his head. Maybe it's the bedlam; maybe it's my diminishing powers. Jake looks happy, but I can tell he's disturbed by my absence. I long to bask in his glory.

I shared much with Christie as we travelled together to Cleveland. I filled her head with more than she probably wanted to know: about Jake, about my post-death adventures. I didn't tell her everything, of course. There's a big difference between ghost stories and skeletons in the closet.

My admiration for Christie has only grown. She endured my admittedly freakish presence with grace. We jabbered like longtime girlfriends—at least when there was no one around to mistake her banter for the ravings of a lunatic. She's not as crazy as I am—or was—but that's to her credit. She's got a great head atop that voluptuous body. She's the perfect woman for my man.

I think I'm done here, though I don't control my destiny. Jake rode a fairy tale dream to the top of the baseball world. It was a glorious trip, and I'm glad I was part of the journey. It was a long time coming. And with Christie, if he plays his cards right, I'm sure he'll find that happiness he so richly deserves. I no longer have the strength or desire to engineer Jake's love life. I've laid down the right signs; it's up to him to deliver the right pitch. Christie's there for the taking, and she's a prize.

I'm weary now. Time escapes me with increasing frequency. I hope, at least, I can say goodbye.

CHAPTER SIXTY-FIVE

Jake

The celebration that began that Wednesday evening continued into the wee hours of Thursday morning. Champagne flowed in rivers through the plastic-draped locker room as we partied like frat boys. Though asleep when I arrived in my apartment at three, Christie rallied, congratulating me in a far different manner. I can't recall a happier day in my life.

Today, Thursday, I soak it all in: our accomplishment, the joy of Christie's presence. She reveals her encounters with Kate—the visitation at Christie's apartment, her 'technical difficulties,' her tales of post-mortem existence. I'd suspected as much, and, had I known Kate's intentions, would have strenuously objected. Yet, I'm grateful for Kate's intercession. She may have mismanaged her own life, but she's always been here for me. I loved her for that, even during the darkest days of our marriage.

"I suggest we keep these spectral conversations to ourselves," I tell Christie.

"I wholeheartedly concur," she says, with a smile. Nick knows of my alleged ghostly encounters, but he's probably long since chalked them up to the shock and pressure of Kate's gruesome death.

In a scene that once seemed preposterous, Christie and I sit on the living room sofa calling Kate's name. Still, she doesn't answer.

"Where in God's name is she?"

"She loses time," Christie says.

The next week is a whirlwind, a circus of celebrations; press conferences; television appearances; radio, newspaper, and magazine interviews. After Christie returns to Tucson, buoyed by the miraculous recovery of her poor, sick aunt, I submit to the inevitable media frenzy. We begin with a parade through the heart of Cleveland—it sounds more appropriate for the losing team—but we have a blast. We ride atop double-deckers to the rousing cheers of the thousands who line the parade route.

For better or worse (mostly worse), I'm in great demand. I fly to New York to do the Letterman show, and to Burbank for *The Tonight Show with Jay Leno.*

"Do you really talk to your late wife on the mound?" Letterman asks.

I give my usual answer—an admission that skirts the surface of the truth. "Of course, she doesn't talk back," I lie. "That'd be a real story," I say, with a chuckle.

Leno's fascination with my mangled left hand veers beyond morbid. Reluctantly, I relate the story of my finger's demise. I imagine wise guys all over New Jersey rushing to claim credit for my maiming.

Photos of Madelyn Moss and me reappear in the tabloids and pepper the internet. I vigorously deny any involvement.

The thrill of attention wears off quickly. After a week, I vow to stem the media tide, forgoing all further appearances and interviews. I close up my Cleveland apartment and return to my empty house in Tucson.

I've come to a crossroads. Technically, my leave of absence from Davis, Davis & Singer is over. Nick indulged me my fantasy and Christie worked day and night to facilitate it. I owe them both.

I ponder my options. Under the complex rules of baseball, I'm under contractual control of the Cleveland Indians for several more years, devoid of leverage. I'll be in my late thirties before I can auction my services to the highest bidder. No rational team will pay handsomely for a pitcher pushing forty. I've had the ride of a lifetime, but can anything match what I've just experienced? And if Kate can't continue the journey, the mound will be a lonelier place.

Even as I grieve the disappearance of Kate, I think about Christie. Is it presumptuous to see her at the heart of my future? Kate didn't think so. But where Kate was mercurial, Christie—like me—is cautious and deliberate. A long-distance romance would be challenging for both of us.

If Kate were present, she wouldn't hesitate to weigh in on my dilemma. I think I know what she'd say.

CHAPTER SIXTY-SIX

Christie

Jake called me immediately upon his return to Tucson. He said he'd made a tentative decision and wanted to know what I thought. I told him. Then he asked me to join him for a press conference in Cleveland. My aunt had conveniently taken ill again, so I packed my bags for the Mistake on the Lake.

The Progressive Park media room is filled to capacity, despite the short notice. At Jake's suggestion, I stand off to one side, out of the glare of the bright lights. As the one o'clock starting time arrives, Jake remains sequestered in a back room with Marty Milano and Indians' General Manager Clay Burton. Reporters murmur among themselves, trying to divine the reason for the conclave. They fear the worst, but 'the worst' varies from reporter to reporter. Finally, Jake and Marty enter together from the door beside me. They take their seats at the podium.

Marty, accustomed to addressing the media, speaks first. "Thank you all for coming," he begins. "Jake has something he wants to say."

Jake reaches for the microphone, drawing it closer as he scans the crowd. He looks uncomfortable. He extracts a scrap of paper from his front pocket and unfolds it. Lights flash as a hush descends over the room.

"As most of you know, this year has been an eventful one for me . . . for a host of reasons." Jake pauses, glancing down at his notes. "While grieving the loss of my wife, I embarked on a long-deferred baseball career with results far surpassing my wildest dreams. It's been a heckuva ride," he says, "and I cherished every moment." Jake exhales deeply. He folds his hands together, resting them on the table by the microphone. I can see tears glistening in those big, blue-gray eyes. "I've decided," he says, haltingly, "to bow out on top."

Some in the room gasp in disbelief. Others look at their neighbors with that self-satisfied expression that suggests that they'd known all along. In either case, the air is heavy with disappointment and regret. The reporters' best story in decades evaporates before their eyes. Jake pauses before continuing.

"I want to thank each of you, the entire city of Cleveland, and Indians' fans everywhere, for embracing and inspiring me. I'll always be grateful."

With that, Jake looks up. Something in the back of the room catches his eye. I direct my gaze to where he's looking. I see what he sees . . . and I can't believe it!

Kate Singer stands in the back of the room. She's smiling sweetly, while wiping tears from her eyes. *Does anyone else see this? Is this real?* Unaware of what's happening, reporters pepper Jake with questions. He fails to respond. His eyes remain fixed on Kate. Tears overcome him. Marty doesn't know what to do, so he reaches over and places an arm awkwardly around Jake's shoulder.

I look back toward Kate. She's waving to Jake. She turns toward me and nods. I glance again at Jake, then retrain my eyes on the back of the room. She's no longer there. Kate's gone. Jake stands up, trying desperately to spot her. Reporters continue to hurl questions his way. It's as if he hears nothing. He turns and walks from the podium, and back through the door through which he entered. I follow him out of the press room.

"Did you see her?" he asks me, weeping unabashedly.

"Yes," I say. "But no one else did. I'm sure of it."

"She's gone, isn't she."

"I think so."

"Picked a hell of a time and place to say goodbye," Jake says, as he tries to regain his composure. "She always had a flair for the dramatic."

I think back to the day of Kate's funeral. Jake couldn't shed a tear. He makes up for it now.

"I'll miss her," he says, his voice shaking.

"I know," I say, "me, too."

He grasps my hand. We walk through the warren of hallways beneath the park, out the stadium exit, and into the sunshine.

—The End—

Acknowledgments

It was in the 1980s, around the time that an obscure writer named W. P. Kinsella penned the inventive, magic realist novel *Shoeless Joe* (better known for its film incarnation as *Field of Dreams*), that baseball fiction had its heyday, when each spring would pour forth a torrent of titles, some good, some less so. It was then that I became enamored of the notion that I might some day write a baseball novel of my own. It would take more than three decades for my dream to come to fruition.

Publishing professionals warned me that baseball novels are passé. Men don't read, the argument goes, and women don't love baseball. But good baseball novels are about more than just baseball—they're about love, loss, redemption, even death. While no more than a game to some, to others—including such literary notables as Bernard Malamud, Philip Roth, and John Grisham—baseball is nothing less than a metaphor for life. I hope that you've enjoyed *Four-Finger Singer and His Late Wife, Kate*, and will recommend it to others, both men and women, fans and non-fans alike.

Writing this book was a labor of love, but one informed and improved by the thoughtful comments and suggestions of a valiant few who were willing to pore through the manuscript, in some cases more than once. My heartfelt thanks to Tim Neely and Ken Brooks, whose enthusiastic support and perceptive critiques have been invaluable; and especially to

Gary Null, a passionate reader and grammarian who rescued me from Bill Bucknerian errors of both baseball and syntax. And to my wife Peggy, who invariably laughs at my attempts at humor and whose encouragement never wavers.

Finally, I thank you, my readers, for taking time out of your busy lives to read what I've written. And if you're so inclined, please consider posting a review online (e.g., Amazon, Goodreads); your support is nectar to independent authors and is always deeply appreciated.

About the Author

ARTHUR D. HITTNER is the author of **Artist, Soldier, Lover, Muse** (Apple Ridge Press, 2017), a critically acclaimed novel about an emerging young artist in New York City during the late Depression and prelude to World War II, and **Honus Wagner: The Life of Baseball's Flying Dutchman** (McFarland Publishing, 1996), recipient of the 1997 Seymour Medal awarded by the Society for American Baseball Research for the best work of baseball biography or history published during the preceding year. He has also written or co-written several art catalogues, a biography and catalogue raisonne on the artist Harold J. Rabinovitz, and articles on American art and artists for national publications including *Fine Art Connoisseur*, *Antiques & Fine Art* and *Maine Antique Digest*.

A retired attorney, Hittner spent nearly thirty-four years with the national law firm now known as Nixon Peabody, resident in the firm's Boston office. He served as a trustee of Danforth Art (formerly the Danforth Museum of Art) in Framingham, Massachusetts and the Tucson Museum of Art in Tucson, Arizona. He was also a co-owner of the Lowell Spinners, a minor league professional baseball team affiliated with his beloved Boston Red Sox.

Married with two children and three grandchildren, Hittner currently divides his time between Oro Valley, Arizona and

Natick, Massachusetts. He is a graduate of Dartmouth College and Harvard Law School.

For additional information about the author's other books, please visit www.hittnerbooks.com.

CPSIA information can be obtained
at www.ICGtesting.com
Printed in the USA
FFHW020648070419
51475518-56953FF